AF660558

SECOND EDITION – EXPANDED AND UPDATED VERSION

THE ULTIMATE MIND TRAINING SYSTEM

THE MIRACLE MINDSET: SIMPLE SECRETS TO HAPPINESS & SUCCESS

GYAN PANPATIL

Clever Fox® PUBLISHING

Chennai • Bangalore

CLEVER FOX PUBLISHING
Chennai, India

Published by CLEVER FOX PUBLISHING 2025
Copyright © Gyan Panpatil 2025

All Rights Reserved.
ISBN: 978-93-6707-455-8

This book has been published with all reasonable efforts taken to make the material error-free after the consent of the author. No part of this book shall be used, reproduced in any manner whatsoever without written permission from the author, except in the case of brief quotations embodied in critical articles and reviews.

The Author of this book is solely responsible and liable for its content including but not limited to the views, representations, descriptions, statements, information, opinions and references ["Content"]. The Content of this book shall not constitute or be construed or deemed to reflect the opinion or expression of the Publisher or Editor. Neither the Publisher nor Editor endorse or approve the Content of this book or guarantee the reliability, accuracy or completeness of the Content published herein and do not make any representations or warranties of any kind, express or implied, including but not limited to the implied warranties of merchantability, fitness for a particular purpose. The Publisher and Editor shall not be liable whatsoever for any errors, omissions, whether such errors or omissions result from negligence, accident, or any other cause or claims for loss or damages of any kind, including without limitation, indirect or consequential loss or damage arising out of use, inability to use, or about the reliability, accuracy or sufficiency of the information contained in this book.

This book is dedicated to my beloved mother

Late Rajas Keshavlal Panpatil

A NOTE TO THE READER

Dear Reader,

This book serves as a roadmap, a supportive friend, and an inspiration to help you discover and activate the vast potential that already exists inside you.But remember—*your journey is uniquely yours.*

Think of this book not as a rulebook, but as a mirror reflecting your own hidden strengths. Take what resonates, practice it sincerely, and adapt it to your own life. Small steps, taken daily, can create transformations far beyond your imagination.

Though the Author himself has benefitted from the techniques provided in this book, it is his own personal journey and your experience may vary. Hence, the Author refrains from making any claims and the book makes no guarantees of specific outcomes or results.

This book is written for educational and motivational purposes only. It does not claim to replace professional advice, whether medical, psychological, or financial. The ideas and practices shared here are meant to inspire positive change, but results may vary based on individual effort and circumstances.Every individual's journey is unique.

While these practices are rooted in timeless wisdom and modern insights, please use your own discretion in applying them. Not every method may suit every reader in every situation, so listen to yourself and adapt accordingly.

Above all, know this: you are capable of more than you realize. Trust the process, trust yourself, and allow your mind to become the ultimate tool for creating the life you truly deserve.

With gratitude and encouragement,

The Author

CONTENTS

PREFACE

Positive Thinking Isn't Going to Help You Succeed in Life!

Yes, you read that right.

This statement might shock you because the shelves of bookstores and the timelines of social media are flooded with self-help gurus chanting, "Be positive! Think positive! Stay positive!" The phrase has become a mantra for life coaches and motivational speakers alike. But here's the hard truth—positive thinking alone will not take you where you want to go.

It reminds me of the famous quote, "Knowledge is power." Sounds inspiring, but it's also incomplete. Knowledge by itself does nothing. Only applied knowledge—knowledge put into meaningful action—unlocks real power. A book that is read but never implemented is no different from a book left unread on a dusty shelf.

The same holds true for positive thinking. You can fill your mind with optimistic thoughts, affirm to yourself that you are capable, and even maintain a sunny smile in the darkest storm—but if these thoughts are never turned into focused action, they remain as harmless and ineffective as steam escaping into thin air.

The Steam Engine Lesson

Take the story of James Watt. It's said that Watt first noticed the power of steam while watching food being cooked in his kitchen. The steam from boiling water pushed the lid off a pot, revealing to him a source of energy that could change the world. And it did—the steam engine became the driving force of the Industrial Revolution.

But here's the key point: that steam was just a potential force until it was captured, channeled, and converted into mechanical motion. Left alone, it would vanish into the air, achieving nothing. Similarly, positive thinking is raw mental energy—it becomes transformative only when harnessed by a system of planning, persistent effort, and disciplined execution.

The Trap of "Feel-Good" Motivation

I've seen people who live in a cloud of cheerful talk, posting inspiring quotes every morning, attending endless workshops, and stacking their shelves with self-help books—yet year after year, their careers, relationships, and financial situations remain exactly the same.

It's not that the books are useless. It's that they treat motivation like a mood rather than a tool. They get a temporary "high" after reading or listening, but since they never anchor that inspiration with action, nothing changes. This is what I call Motivational Entertainment. It feels good, but it doesn't build your future.

It's like buying expensive gym clothes and watching workout videos on YouTube without ever stepping on the treadmill. The intention is there. The enthusiasm is there. But the action is missing.

Life Rewards Action, Not Intention

If you find yourself stuck despite being "positive" and "ambitious," it's worth asking:

Am I actually moving toward my goal, or am I just thinking about moving?

I once met a man who dreamed of starting his own business. He spent years talking about it, reading about it, and imagining the freedom it would bring. But he never registered a company, never built a product, and never even made his first sale. His dream remained anchored to the dock, much like the story of the man who sat in a boat gazing at the riches across the sea but refused to untie the rope for fear of the journey. Until you cut that rope—your fear, your excuses, your hesitation—you'll never sail to the other shore.

Cut the rope that is holding you back. Take this one firm step.

A tiny seed may look ordinary in your palm, yet it holds within it the possibility of growing into a mighty tree..

But left on the table, it will never touch the soil.

Your mind is the same.

Positive thinking is only the seed—it needs the water of action.

Ambition Alone Isn't Enough

In youth, ambition burns brightly. We want to conquer the world. But over time, ambition quietly gets replaced by "adjustments" and "practical compromises."

Why? Because ambition without a clear goal, a detailed plan, and disciplined effort is like a car with no fuel. It looks good but goes nowhere.

The ego loves ambition because it's flattering—it makes us feel special without having to do the work. But true success comes from pairing ambition with action and facing the obstacles on the way. As the Zen proverb says,"Obstacles don't block the path. They are the path."

My Own Turning Point

For many years, I carried within me the desire to write a book.. But deadlines, job pressures, and excuses kept me from starting. Then in 2015, I was posted to a workplace that required a four-hour round-trip daily. I could have complained about the commute. Instead, I turned that time into my writing lab. I observed people. I reflected on my own thoughts and emotions. Bit by bit, the first version of this book began to emerge..

Years later, in 2021, I was posted 550 kilometers away from my family. Again, there were times when solitude could have crushed me, but I chose not to give in and instead chose to use solitude for creative work—completing this book, developing new training programs, and designing courses that would one day give me financial freedom. Challenges can either imprison us or empower us. It's always our choice.

Your Mental Clutter Is Your Responsibility

We say that life is a struggle. But, most of the time, the struggle is because of a lack of effort. What efforts have you taken so far to improve your present situation? We put in no effort and then call it a struggle. The important thing is to start. Don't be stagnant, move and initiate action.

Suppose you have moved into a new house and there is lots of cleaning to be done and clutter to be arranged; what would you do?

Will you just sit back and look at the mess because clearing and arranging it is a time-consuming and tedious job?

You will work on it because there is no other option, as you have to stay in that house. In that case, you will start from somewhere and move from one item to another. Step by step, the disorder begins to settle as your mind naturally directs you toward clarity. Eventually, the work is done and everything falls into place.

The same can be said of our lives. We create mental clutter, which causes issues and barriers. We do nothing and then sit back and stare at the shambles. Nobody else is going to clean up after you. Get up and take that one courageous step forward. If you're focused and motivated, your brain will lead you through the rest of the process.

Life works the same way. Mental clutter—fear, doubt, procrastination—won't clean itself. Nobody else can take this step on your behalf.. You must start, even if you don't see the whole path. Take the first step, and your brain will guide you to the next.

The Essence of This Book

If you underline only one sentence from this book, make it this:

"We live our lives in our minds."

Our thinking patterns—not our circumstances—create the majority of our struggles.

Shift the way you think, and the entire course of your life shifts with it.

This book will guide you to train your mind through habit formation, perspective shifts, and practical exercises so that your thoughts become a launchpad for action rather than a substitute for it.

We often say "life is a struggle," but in truth, life is an opportunity disguised as a challenge. The real struggle is not against circumstances but against our own inertia. You have the tools. You have the potential. Now all that remains is the courage to begin.

Start. Move. Act.

Your future self is waiting.

Passing thought

All along, you've heard the advice to keep a **positive** mindset..

But if positive thinking was the key to success, wouldn't we all be living our dream lives by now? The truth is harsher—thinking alone won't move you forward.

It's like sitting in a boat, staring at the horizon, but refusing to untie the rope.

This chapter isn't here to make you feel good.

It's here to push you into the water so you finally start rowing.

The world doesn't reward thoughts.

It rewards actions that turn thoughts into reality.

This book will challenge your comfort zone.

Because you don't need more positivity—you need movement.

You've kept delaying, hoping for the "perfect moment" to begin..

Months turned to years. Your dreams are still waiting.

You tell yourself to stay hopeful. You keep your spirits high.

But deep inside, you know—hope without action is just delay in disguise.

This book is your wake-up call.

Because your dreams are tired of waiting.

This book isn't about wishful thoughts.

It's about planting, watering, and growing your future.

Continue with a happy reading. May you be blessed and happy!

CHAPTER I

THE END

"If we don't know life, how can we know death?
We have two lives, and the second begins when
we realise we have only one."

– Confucius

Don't be surprised by seeing THE END at the very start of a book.

Because that is where our life's story will ultimately take us—to death.

This is not meant to frighten you but to wake you up.

Every page you read hereafter is a reminder that our time is limited—and that proper use of the concepts in this book can help you not only remove the fear of death but also live more fully, achieve more in your career and relationships, enjoy better health, create wealth, and grow spiritually within this single, short lifetime.

Death is the most certain event in life, and yet the most ignored.

And perhaps, that's our greatest mistake.

The Emperor's Lesson

I once heard a story about an emperor—a wise, benevolent, and disciplined ruler—whose younger brother was the exact opposite. The younger man was lost in indulgence, chasing pleasure without responsibility, ignoring his duties toward the people.

Eager to stir him from his slumber, the emperor crafted a plan. One day, while his brother was bathing, soldiers quietly replaced his clothes with the royal robes of the emperor. Tempted, the brother put them on in secret. At that very moment, the emperor appeared and, feigning outrage, accused him of treason—an act equal to usurping the throne.

As punishment, the emperor sentenced him to death. However, he offered a strange mercy: the younger brother could live as emperor for one full week before execution, free to indulge in every desire.

The week passed. When the moment of execution arrived, the emperor inquired,

"Did you enjoy your week as emperor?"

His brother sighed,

"How could I enjoy it when death was hanging over me every moment?"

The emperor smiled.

"That, dear brother, is the human condition. Death hangs over each of us. Yours was announced, while others live pretending it isn't there. But in truth, it could come for any of us—today, tomorrow, or years from now."

Then, revealing that the death sentence was only a plan to reform, the emperor urged his brother to live a meaningful life from that day forward.

Life Is Preparation for Death

Whatever we do in life—our work, relationships, dreams, and habits—is ultimately preparation for the moment we leave it. At the time of death, the sum of our choices decides whether we depart with peace or with regret.

If life has been a celebration, death too can be a celebration. But if we've spent our days only chasing distractions, avoiding purpose, or postponing joy, the end becomes terrifying.

Life is available right here, right now—this very moment. The question is: Are we truly living it?

The Journey Analogy: Why Are We Born?

Let's take an example of a train journey. You board at Station B, and your destination is Station D.

Along the way, you can fill the time however you like—reading, enjoying the view, eating snacks, making new friends, or simply staring out the window. These activities can be pleasant or unpleasant, but they are secondary. Your prime objective is still to reach your destination.

Similarly, in life, what matters most is not the little distractions along the way, but how meaningfully you travel toward the inevitable end. The way you manage your time during this journey determines whether you arrive from station B (Birth) to Station D (Death) with peace or with panic.

Why Do We Fear Death?

Death is not something to be feared—it is the one certainty we often choose to forget. When it finally approaches, fear grips us, not because of death itself, but because our journey through life feels incomplete. We have unfulfilled dreams, dear ones to lose, scores to settle, and things to achieve, causing anxiety at the time of death. Very few of us face death happily because we ignore it when alive and fill up our time with useless stuff or inactivity. When the end comes, we fail to have adequately lived. At the time of death, we don't ask for an empire or riches but crave a few more moments of life. We want life to stay on. But alas, life is not going to wait. The same life force that animates us now is here, in this very moment. Let's cherish it. Let's live it to the fullest. So, don't wait till the end or till you get old. Why wait for illness, old age, or "the right time" to begin living?

Start now and live before you leave

A person whose death is beautiful has, without exception, lived a beautiful life.

So, Why Are We Born?

The simplest answer is: to die.

But the nature of our death will always mirror the way we have lived

Exercise- feeling the Pulse of Life

This exercise, often used in my live training sessions, can be profoundly moving. At home, do it in solitude.

Imagine you are sitting comfortably in a quiet hall. The speaker's voice is calm and deep. He says:"Close your eyes"

"Take a deep breath… and relax. Observe the breath as it enters and exits the nostrils.

Feel the chest rise and fall naturally.

Notice the heartbeat—steady, rhythmic.

I'm blessed because the body is still breathing,

I'm blessed because the heart is still beating,

I'm blessed because the body and mind are still functioning.

I'm profoundly blessed because….. Because the life energy is still flowing through my body.

I'm Alive. What can be a greater feeling than being alive?

Being alive is the only criterion; everything else can be achieved. Life and the lost moments cannot be reclaimed.

Pause for a moment and realise—you are alive right now. This is the most noteworthy thing ever.

This life energy flowing through you is not ordinary—it is the same force that powers oceans, moves the planets, births the stars, and sustains the entire universe.

And right now, it has chosen you as its vessel.

If such a vast and creative energy is flowing within you, why doubt your ability to achieve health, love, abundance, and success? Why believe your problems are bigger than the power that created galaxies?

The truth is—this energy already holds the solutions. The challenge is learning how to channel it.

Life is always ready to offer you plenty, but the key lies in knowing how to ask for it—and how to move towards it.

As long as you are alive, limitless possibilities remain open to you.

The greatest qualification for success is simply… being here, now.

Closing Truth

A person is lying on a hospital bed. The beeping of the heart monitor is slowing. The room smells faintly of antiseptic and fading flowers. His loved ones stand around, some crying, some holding his hand. His breath is shallow. In the seconds between each inhale and exhale, one thought pierces through every memory, every achievement, and every regret: "I wish I had lived more."

"We have two lives, and the second begins when we realize we only have one." — Confucius

Death changes our perspective in an instant. Suddenly, promotions, social media likes, or the latest gadgets mean nothing. What counts are the moments we truly experienced.

Yet most of us move through life as if we have an unlimited supply of tomorrows. We save our real dreams for "someday." We stay stuck in jobs, relationships, and routines that drain us—telling ourselves we're "being responsible" when in reality, we're just afraid.

Here's a reality most people avoid saying aloud:

Life doesn't pause for you to get ready. The clock has been ticking since the moment you were born.

When you realize that, you stop waiting for the perfect conditions. You stop obsessing over what people think. You finally stop delaying your real life.

It's not about reckless living—it's about conscious urgency. Choosing to act while you have breath, health, and energy. Choosing to take that trip, write that book, start that business, say "I love you" before it's too late.

The end will come for all of us. The only question is whether we will meet it with satisfaction or with the taste of "what if" still on our tongues.

May you be blessed with both clarity of thought and the fire of action.

CHAPTER 2

TIMING THE TIME

"You may delay, but time will not."

– Benjamin Franklin

The Illusion of Tomorrow

We live as if "tomorrow" is a guarantee.

We treat it like an invisible savings account in which we can deposit all the things we don't feel like doing today—our dreams, our health, and our relationships.

We tell ourselves:

I'll start the business later.

I'll plan that trip next year.

I'll get that house when the moment truly aligns.

I'll spend more time with my loved ones once things settle down.

But here's the truth—while you wait for tomorrow, you are ageing.

Your energy changes. Your health changes. Your mind changes.

Life throws in accidents, illnesses, tragedies, and unexpected responsibilities.

And time? It just keeps moving—quietly, steadily, without pausing to see if you're ready.

By the time you realise it's slipping away, it's already gone.

Do It Now. Get Moving.

The only moment you truly own is now.

So instead of postponing, start today:

- Plan for riches now.
- Plan for that dream home now.
- Plan for that dream car now.
- Plan for vacations now.
- Plan something special for your loved ones now.

Because somebody once said it perfectly, ***"Postpone your dreams and they expire."***

Wealth, Freedom & Time

Chasing your dreams isn't just about earning money—it's about reclaiming your time and creating freedom..

- Earn riches in a time-bound way – think beyond the standard 10–6 job.

- There's abundant wealth in the world; prepare yourself to claim your share.
- Wealth creation isn't tied to your educational degree—it's tied to your ability to adapt, innovate, and spot opportunities.
- Let your wealth grow for you—invest it smartly so you're not chained to every paycheck.
- Retire early while your body is still strong. Retire from what drains you, but keep working on what excites you.
- Dedicate time to your passions—travel, hobbies, and learning.
- Spend real quality time with your loved ones—without screens, without hurry.
- Give back—through charity, mentorship, or service. The joy of selfless giving is unmatched.
- Nurture your spiritual self—not with superstition, but with an understanding of the universal principles that bring calm and harmony within..

Why We Fail to 'Time' the Time, Our biggest mistake?

We think of time as something that moves at a fixed, predictable speed—like the ticking of a clock.

But time is relative.

Recall your childhood, days stretched endlessly, and summers felt infinite.

In your teenage years, time felt faster.

By adulthood, weeks start disappearing.

By old age, years vanish like months.

This isn't just perception—it's a reflection of how our mind processes life.

When we don't match our actions to the true pace of time, it slips away before we realise it.

The division of time into hours, minutes, and seconds is a human convenience—it doesn't capture the real speed at which life passes.

And here's the brutal truth: you will never feel like you "have time."

The clock will never say, "Now it's perfect to start."

Life is a moving river.

If you drift without direction, the tide will pull you toward places you never planned to reach.

The problem is not a lack of time—

It's lack of urgency, focus, and conscious use of the time we have.

Your goals, your dreams, your relationships—

All of them are on a timer, whether you acknowledge it or not.

And the timer is counting down.

Power Reminder

Time will pass anyway—whether you act or not.

The question is:

Will you look back and see a collection of excuses?

Or a collection of fulfilled dreams?

The choice is yours.

And the time is now.

CHAPTER 3

RETIRE EARLY & LIVE YOUR LIFE

Though 'livelihood' contains the term 'live', earning of livelihood should not be a lifelong process!

At the outset of this chapter, let me be clear: retirement does not imply inaction. On the contrary, it is a period in which one appreciates what they are doing. In a nutshell, it's about living life according to one's preferences. An inspired, lively life is one where you earn by doing what excites you most. As the old wisdom goes, when you love your work, it never feels like labor. Retirement should be from the activities or jobs we no longer enjoy. It is not about being lazy in retirement; it is about reinventing yourself.

Our mindset, which considers retirement an old age phenomenon, needs to be changed; it is possible to retire in our prime. This will give us more time to live life rather than just spending it. Therefore, if we want to live this short life span to the fullest, a strategy to start early and retire early is needed. The journey begins with creating financial stability. The wealth creation plan consists of earning money and proper investing. The earlier we start, the more we gain due to the compounding effect. The only condition is to remain determined and consistent in our efforts towards achieving our goals during the designated period and start investing at the earliest. Most of us are aware of the concept of compounding or have at least heard about its significance. Let's understand this through an example.

Example of Compounding Riches

Vijay gave a loan of Rs. 20 Lakhs (two million) to his close friend Vimal, who set up a successful business venture but avoids repaying the loan amount on one pretext or another. Since there is no written evidence about the payment, Vijay gets depressed and eventually confides in his wife, Preeti. A professional banker, Preeti, meets Vimal and politely asks the reason for not refunding the loan amount. Nervous, Vimal tries to reason out and asks for some extra time for repayment. Preeti gives him a simple option to repay in instalments. Vimal cannot resist the visibly lucrative option and agrees in writing to pay as per the following terms;

The payment is to be made for 30 days only. It involves paying Rs.1 on day one and doubling the amount every day till the 30th day. This means paying Rs. 1 on day 1, paying Rs. 2 (double of Rs.1) on day 2, paying Rs.4 (double of Rs. 2) on day 3, paying Rs. 16 (double of Rs. 4) on the fourth day, and continuing in this way for the entire 30-day period.

The payment in this manner is to be made for 30 days only. Vimal was thrilled as he thought that he would be repaying a much lesser amount than Rs. 20 Lakhs that he had borrowed.

This payment arrangement looks totally in favour of Vimal, right?

Wrong!

Though the amount during the initial days looks meagre, it increases exponentially as it approaches the 30th day. The amount is exorbitantly higher than what Vimal was supposed to repay. Do this exercise. Take out a pen and paper or prepare an Excel sheet to calculate the amount payable, and you will be astonished to know the result. Vimal will have to pay much, much more than what he has imagined.

This example also applies to investing and wealth creation. Start with a smaller amount, add to it regularly, and stay invested in creating an unimaginable fortune over time.

The earlier you start and the more prolonged the duration of investment, the higher the wealth created.

Let us understand this through one more example. We all learned about compound interest formulas during our schooling. Let's revisit that formula. Relax, it's actually quite simple. Also, you need to know about it to understand your future projected investments and returns. A few minutes to understand this may change your life.

Even Warren Buffett accepts "compound interest" as the single most powerful factor behind his investing success. He's been preaching this for nearly six decades, and it's made him a billionaire.

The general expression for compound interest is $A = P (1 + r/n)^{(nt)}$, where P is the principal amount, r is the rate of interest, n is the number of times interest is compounded per year, and t is the number of time periods.

Let us further simplify this formula by considering that the compounding is annual (i.e. done once a year). If interest is compounded just once annually, the formula reduces to: $A = P (1 + r)^t$

The Numbers Don't Lie

Example: Two brothers, A and B, each inherit Rs. 5,00,000.

- A invests for 10 years at 10% interest.
- B invests for 20 years at the same rate.
- For A: Rs. 5,00,000 × (1 + 0.1)^10 = Rs. 12,96,871
- For B: Rs. 5,00,000 × (1 + 0.1)^20 = Rs. 33,63,750

Same amount, same rate—yet B ends up with 2.6 times more, simply because he stayed invested twice as long.

"Compound interest is like a silent architect—it builds wealth brick by brick, rewarding patience and discipline, while punishing neglect."

Passing Thought

The earlier you start investing, the more your money works for you—not just once, but again and again, like a tree producing fruit, and those fruits producing seeds for more trees.

So, start early and stay invested longer. One of the aims of this book is remind the readers not to delay. Start with whatever resources you have.

CHAPTER 4

BEGIN FROM WITHIN

The universe is not outside of you. Look inside yourself. Ask all from yourself- Rumi

So, you want to get rich, retire early, and sort out those problems in your life, but don't know where to begin! The starting point for attaining our goals lies within us. Outside success is nothing but a reflection of our inner conditioning. Move inside to succeed outside.

A beautiful story can explain this,

Once saddened by his failures, a man decides to visit one of the Buddhist monasteries in a remote mountainous region. The serene climate and tranquil atmosphere fail to lift his mood. A monk notices his plight and asks him to attend meditation sessions. Unable to concentrate, he leaves the session midway and sits beside a lake. As the monk walks up and sits beside him, the man confesses to not being able to meditate. The monk smiles and assures him of a simpler meditation technique. The monk points to a small debris by the lake and tells him to remove it and see what happens. The man gets down, removing the accumulated weeds, plant waste, and pebbles with his hands. As he attentively keeps working, suddenly a gush of stream emerges from beneath the debris. Excitedly, he clears all the obstacles from the stream's path and watches as the stream flows splendidly into the lake. A calm sensation prevails within him as his mind consciously observes the movement of the stream.

The monk, who till then was calmly observing the man, now speaks his words of wisdom,

"Dear friend, the stream of water was clogged and its movement was restricted due to the debris. Though the stream was not visible due to the debris, it still existed beneath it. Similarly, the stream of bliss exists inside every one of us, hidden due to the negative emotions that clog it. We need to work diligently to clear this burden of negative emotions to get a glimpse of the eternal bliss that lies within us; it always exists, waiting to be explored. How can we expect to attain happiness when the emotions of fear, anxiety, hatred, and depression have taken control of our inner selves?"

It is, therefore, very important to understand the nature of our inner self (conditioning). The more negative emotions we hold inside, the more problems we create for ourselves. Do you want to explore the internal conditioning of your mind? Try the following exercise.

Exercise :

This exercise helps us to understand our inner composition and what lies within.

Close your eyes and be very sincere with your observation.

Start from the present moment onwards and move back into the past. Try to recollect the negative acts and emotions that happened in your life in the recent past. Try to recollect those emotions of anger, argument, sadness, jealousy, hatred, fear, helplessness, etc., that happened today, yesterday, the day before, and so on. Go back into the past as much as your mind can take you . Do this for 2- 3 minutes.

Once you are done with this activity, wait for a few seconds and carry out the same exercise for past positive acts and emotions. Try to recollect the moments of positive acts and emotions that happened in your life in the recent past. Try to recall those emotions of happiness, love, and bliss that happened today, yesterday, the day before, and so on. Go back in the past as much as your mind can take you. Do this for 2- 3 minutes.

What is your realization? You will realise that the negative emotions far outnumber the positive ones. You could easily remember the negative moments, but the positive moments were difficult to find.

Isn't it a contradiction that our inner self is filled with garbage of negative emotions, and we still wonder about the reasons for all those horrible things happening in our lives? When our inner self is full of negativity, how can we expect positive things to happen?

Ever wondered why you are poor or debt-ridden? Why do you have health issues? Why do you have relationship issues? Why do failures, sorrow, heartbreaks and all those problems in life surround you, and there are very few sunshine moments?

The simple thing we fail to understand is that our outer world is nothing but the reflection of our inner happenings & conditioning. No one else but we are responsible for the mess that is affecting our outside outcomes.

The negativity that we carry inside us is the cause of all our problems. The vast proportion of negativity inside us overwhelms the very few positive emotions. This is the leading cause of all our problems.

According to the National Science Foundation and published in Mission.org, an average person has about 12,000 to 60,000 thoughts per day. Of those, 80% are negative, and 95% are repetitive thoughts. How can someone burdened with an endless cycle of negative thoughts truly feel happiness? It is indeed a tough challenge, and overcoming it requires conscious effort and practice.

How to deal with negative emotions

Let's take the example of anger. What happens to this anger energy after we express it? A person may scream or use foul language to vent their anger. So, will this make the energy be thrown out of his system?

No! Screaming or being furious doesn't unburden us. On the contrary, it disturbs us from within. The energy rises and settles down within our system, thereby forming layers of it over the years. This causes conditioning or habit formation. The older we grow, the more easily we get irritated or become angry. We develop a short temper. The short temper is not a matter of a single day but has happened due to repeated mental reactions.

Two Golden Principles for Dealing with Emotions

As per the law of physics, energy cannot be created or destroyed: it can only be transformed. Similarly, the energy generated due to anger or any other emotions cannot be destroyed or removed from our system. It can only be converted into a neutral form of energy.

The question is, how to change this habit pattern or convert this potent negative energy to neutral?

For the time being, understand the following two facts about dealing with emotions, and it will be easier to deal with them.

- Never fight with your emotions. Fighting emotions is like fighting a quagmire (quicksand). The more you fight, the more you will sink into it.
- Emotions are nothing but a form of energy that can be converted into another form. Negative energy can thus be transformed into positive or neutral energy.

Reflection Thought

Suppressing or battling emotions is never the true solution. When we resist them, they often return with greater force, leaving us feeling even more trapped. The real key lies in transforming these emotions into a more constructive form.

For example, anger, when redirected, can fuel determination to bring about positive change; sadness, when expressed through writing or art, can turn into healing and self-discovery.

The mind, however, does not change instantly. Its conditioning has been built over many years—through repeated thoughts, beliefs, and experiences. Just as it takes time to unlearn a habit or strengthen a weak muscle, reshaping the mind requires patience, steady effort, and compassion toward oneself. With consistent practice, what once felt like an emotional burden can become a source of strength, clarity, and growth.

CHAPTER 5

CHANGING THE THOUGHT PATTERN

All that we are is the result of what we have thought

–Buddha

We are the product of our thought process. Every creation begins as a thought, and each thought arises within the mind.. It is therefore important to mind the 'Mind' where the formations of beliefs take place. To understand the basis of our beliefs, we first need to be sincere with ourselves.

Ego or Willpower

The first step is to learn to distinguish between ego and willpower. A person may wonder why, despite possessing tremendous willpower, they have failed to achieve greater things in life. We unknowingly consider the ego as a willpower or determination. In such a case, we are most likely to fail because the ego is blind. It doesn't understand what is right or wrong. It's an opposing force that creates a haze in our minds. Will power, on the other hand, is a positive force that is governed by practical thinking. Will power determines self-belief, and self-belief is the primary and initial starting point of success. A doubt-free mind with a goal and a plan to achieve that goal enhances willpower.

Ego, on the other hand, is dangerous as it makes us jump to a conclusion without a proper goal or planning. I have seen people who gave up their jobs just because of overconfidence about their ability (due to ego) and then failing miserably. Many other people leave their job and are more successful than before. This is because they knew what they would be doing. They had the goal and the plan in place. Hence, please try to understand if your decisions are being governed by ego or willpower. If it is ego, then ensure that the same is replaced by willpower.

Once you understand how to differentiate between the role of ego and will power in success, the next step is to check self-belief.

Exercise to Check Self-Belief

Let's begin with a simple question—one that I often ask during my training sessions:

"Have you achieved something worth mentioning in your life? If yes, raise your hand." Almost every time, only a few hands go up with certainty.. The rest hesitate, exchange awkward glances, or keep their hands in their laps.

Some look confused.

Some look almost embarrassed.

And many silently think: "No… I haven't done anything great."

This isn't a rare response—it's the story of most people in the world.

Not because they've never achieved anything, but because they've stopped believing in themselves.

The Question That Changes Everything

Let's return to that question—"Have you achieved something worth mentioning in your life?—and this time, let's answer it honestly, without judgment.

Think about the beginning of your life.

A baby starts its journey by crawling, then learns to stand and then walk.

It falls, again and again, sometimes crying, sometimes laughing—but never once thinking, "Maybe walking isn't for me."

The same child learns to speak, trying over and over to copy the sounds made by its parents. Mistakes don't bother the child. Criticism doesn't stop the child. Nature itself pushes the child forward with an inner urge to grow, explore, and survive.

In those early years, you—yes, you—were fearless, unstoppable, and brimming with confidence.

You learned to walk.

You learned to talk.

You learned to eat, play, communicate, and express your needs—all without anyone having to convince you that it was possible.

This was self-belief in its purest form.

It was not taught to you; it was born in you.

The Shift That Changed Everything

But as we grew older, something shifted.

The voice of nature within us—the quiet, powerful inner guide—was gradually drowned out by the noise of the outside world:

Parents, teachers, relatives, society… all telling us what we can and cannot do.

Our innocence, playfulness, and fearlessness began to fade.

In their place came anxiety, fear of failure, self-doubt, and comparison.

The cheerful, unstoppable child became a cautious, nervous adult.

Now, try learning a new language, sport, or musical instrument as an adult. Suddenly, it feels difficult, doesn't it? But as a child, you learned far more complex skills—walking, speaking, understanding—without even realizing it was hard.

Why?

Because the child listens to nature's inner voice, not the world's outer noise.

Rewriting the Story

The truth is, you have already achieved extraordinary things in life.

You've overcome challenges that, at the time, felt impossible—just like learning to walk once was.

So here's your first step toward self-belief:

Repeat to yourself every day:

"I am an achiever."

Say it until the words no longer feel strange.

Say it until your mind stops arguing.

Because here's the reality—believing you're a failure is just as absurd and untrue as believing you've achieved nothing.

Self-belief is a seed called faith. When planted and nurtured, it grows into the unshakable conviction that you can—and will—rise again.

The One Thing in Your Way

The only thing standing between you and your natural, unstoppable energy… is your mind.

A child's mind is uncluttered—it focuses naturally.

As adults, we've piled up blockages: anger, fear, jealousy, hatred, and insecurity.

This debris blocks the flow of our inner power, just like stones and weeds block a stream.

To live fully again, you must clear the path.

You must return to your natural state.

You must remember that at your core—you are pure energy.

Not ordinary energy. Divine energy.

And when you tap into it, life changes in ways you cannot yet imagine.

Fuel for the Journey

It can be said that the one person who interferes with your progress is none other than you. This is because of our self-limiting viewpoint, ego, and false beliefs. The primary and most crucial step towards achieving greater things in life is self-belief, and the good news is that it can be developed. There is ample evidence to prove that people with little or no formal education have achieved tremendous success and riches through sheer effort and their ability to believe in themselves. Remember,

Knowledge has limitations while wisdom knows no boundaries, and our aim should be to develop the latter.

CHAPTER 6

UNDERSTANDING THE UNIVERSAL POWER WITHIN

The universe is not outside of you. Look inside yourself. Ask all from yourself

– Rumi

You may remember the story from an earlier chapter—the sad man, the monk, and the hidden stream buried under debris.

But that story didn't quite end there.

The liberated stream merged with the lake, releasing tiny bubbles that skipped playfully across the surface before fading beneath the water..

The monk, still seated beside the man, watched the bubbles for a moment and continued his teaching.

The Parable of the Bubbles

"Do you know how these water bubbles are formed? Impurities in the lake water are responsible for bubble formation. Bubbles are nothing but a part of the stream water, but due to impurities, it take the form of a bubble and appears to be different from the lake water. Now, if we supposedly induce life into those bubbles and give them an individual mind, then what will happen? The bubbles will start believing themselves as separate entities; they will consider themselves different from other bubbles and the lake. Yet in truth, those bubbles are not separate—they are simply expressions of the lake itself. The bubble can only understand its authentic self by giving away its bubble form and merging into water.

Similarly, we humans are nothing but this incredible universe. Just like bubbles, we too exist due to the internal impurities that we carry. But due to our different forms and individual minds, we fail to recognize ourselves as a part of this whole and start behaving as individuals. The universal force is all-encompassing and is over us, around us, within us, waiting with open arms to help us. This whole existence, including you and me, is born from this great ocean of universal energy. Hence, our aim should be to minimize our internal impurities and return to our pure state of universal consciousness.

Thus, the first step in realising the relationship between ourselves and the universe is to understand that everything around us (including us) is not different from the universe. The universe is nothing but a huge ocean of energy, and everything has arisen from it. Everything is energy.

The famous Einstein equation E=mc2 explains the interrelationship between energy (E) and matter (m). The universe is nothing but a huge factory where this change process from energy to matter and vice versa is continuously happening. Energy remains one, though it reveals itself through many shapes and appearances. This means that everything we see—stars, trees, bodies, thoughts—is simply energy manifesting in different forms.

Why do we have problems in our lives?

As in the above case, impurity is responsible for bubbles; similarly, our existence is also due to the emotional impurities that our unguarded mind accumulates, leading to sanskaras (conditioning). As per the law of inertia, as we learn in physics, a body or thing maintains its state of rest until acted upon by an external force. The bubble in a lake or an ocean has the tendency to maintain its form but eventually loses itself due to air and water pressure and merges with the lake to attain its true state, which is nothing but water. Similarly, nature tries to shake us and awaken us to give up our inner impurities to realise our true divine nature beyond the realm of the mind. Problems in life are nothing but a wake-up call from the natural forces to purify our inner selves.

As per the law of physics, we humans, too, tend to maintain our bodily existence and conditioning, thereby resisting the changes that nature wants us to undergo for our benefit. Our life problems are nothing but nature's way of reminding us to realise our true selves and give up our impurities. Since we have gradually drifted away from the pure state, our inner consciousness tries to shake us to regain that original pure state, and hence, the problems occur. We are unable to understand nature's way and therefore suffer. The problems in our lives are nothing but nature's way of reminding us to purify and clean up the mess within and realise the pure state of existence.

A wake-up call

Everything—including you—is made of the same energy.

The universe is not some faraway place—it is over you, around you, and within you.

You are not a visitor here. You are the universe experiencing itself in human form.

Go back to the bubble in the lake—it exists only because of impurities. In the same way, the impurities in our inner world—negative emotions, limiting beliefs, and mental conditioning (sanskaras)—create a false sense of separation from our source.

Physics teaches us the law of inertia: an object remains in its current state until an external force acts upon it. Likewise, we cling to our conditioned ways of thinking, holding onto our "bubble identity," resisting the transformation nature is trying to bring.

Problems, then, are not punishments.

They are pressured from the ocean, trying to burst the bubble so it can return to its natural state.

Every challenge in your life—every loss, every frustration, every failure—is nature's way of shaking you awake.

It is the universe whispering:

"Drop what is false. Remember who you are."

We suffer because we mistake this shake for cruelty rather than compassion.

Nature is not trying to harm us—it is trying to free us from the prison of our own conditioning.

The moment you dissolve the illusion of separation, you realize—you were the universe all along.

CHAPTER 7

TUNING WITH NATURE

Our ignorance that we are separate from nature
is the greatest cause of our suffering.

Let's understand how the universal cosmic energy and our existence are interconnected and how this energy can be tapped for outstanding achievements.

We often forget a simple yet profound truth: we are not apart from nature. The universal cosmic energy that flows through the rivers, dances in the wind, and fuels the stars is the same energy that breathes within us. When we live in harmony with it, life flows smoothly. When we go against it, we suffer.

Let's explore how this cosmic connection works and how it can be harnessed for extraordinary living.

Nature Is Neutral — But Our Thoughts Shape the Outcome

Look at the laws of nature: they treat everyone equally. Water quenches the thirst of a saint and a sinner alike. Air doesn't ask for your qualifications before letting you breathe. Sunlight does not decide who deserves its warmth.

In the same way, whether it appears as wind, flowing water, or electricity- energy itself carries no bias—it remains neutral.. It doesn't carry moral labels like good or bad. Electricity, for example, can light up a home or electrocute someone. The choice of use lies entirely with us.

The cosmic energy within us works in the same way. It simply facilitates the outcome of our thoughts and intentions. The quality of those thoughts — whether pure or destructive — shapes what manifests in our lives.

Think of your mind as soil, and your thoughts as seeds. The earth does not choose between seeds; it nurtures whatever is sown into it. If you sow seeds of peace, compassion, and possibility, that's what will grow. If you plant seeds of fear, greed, and resentment, that's what will grow too.

Why We Suffer — Disconnection from Nature

Look around — every creature except humans lives in tune with nature. A bird does not resist the changing seasons, and a flower does not rush its bloom—they both trust life's timing. They follow the natural process of evolution. But what about humans? We want to control nature, we are losing our synchronization—our touch with nature.

Imagine Earth without human interference. The rivers would flow cleaner, the forests would grow denser, the skies would remain clearer. Life would run on nature's timeless rhythm. But our technological progress, while making the outside world more comfortable, has often pulled us further away from this natural balance.

No wonder people who live closer to nature — in villages, forests, or mountains — often enjoy greater peace of mind and lower stress levels than city dwellers surrounded by concrete and constant noise.

Why We Stay Distracted?

Our ancestors lived under wide skies, among towering trees and endless landscapes. That vastness naturally drew their minds outward. Even today, our attention is often captured by what's "out there" — the big picture, the dramatic events, the dazzling spectacles. Our forest dwelling ancestors were in awe of nature, trying to understand the surroundings, it was their natural tendency. We carry forward that tendency to focus on outside world causing the mind to remain distracted.

But here's the truth: life's answers can't be found outside. They are often in the tiniest details — the micro-world inside and around us.

Who Created This World?-The Power of Observing the Small

We often ask, who created this world? Our eyes instinctively turn upward, searching the skies for answers, hoping to catch a glimpse of some grand architect at work. But the truth often hides in the opposite direction—not in the vast heavens, but in the smallest, most overlooked corners of existence.

If you want to understand human health, you don't just observe a person from afar—you study their cells, DNA, and the intricate systems working silently within. In the same way, if you wish to grasp the mystery of life, you can learn it from the tiniest life forms.

Take something as humble as the fungus that appears on a forgotten slice of bread. At first, it seems to emerge from nowhere—one day the bread is fresh, the next it is covered in a delicate bloom. No divine hand placed it there; instead, the right environmental factors—moisture, warmth, and time—created the perfect conditions for life to appear.

By simply being curious and observant, you can watch its entire journey: the invisible beginning, the slow and steady growth, the peak of maturity, and the inevitable decay. This tiny drama mirrors the universal cycle of all living things—birth, growth, decline, and transformation. The more we notice such patterns in small things, the closer we come to understanding the grand patterns of the cosmos.

A young monk once asked his teacher, "Master, who created life?"

The teacher did not reply with words. Instead, he handed the monk a bowl of rice and asked him to leave it in a dark corner for a few days. When the monk returned, the rice was covered with mold.

The teacher asked, "Did you notice anyone arriving to put this here?" The monk shook his head.

"Then how did it grow?" the teacher asked.

"The air, the moisture, and the warmth made it happen," the monk replied.

The teacher smiled. "Exactly. Life unfolds when the conditions are right. The creator is not always a person—it is the harmony of forces, seen and unseen, working together in perfect balance."

Likewise, if you want peace and clarity, you need to move away from larger picture outside and move inside by observing your mind — its patterns, its habits, its conditioning. By understanding the micro-structure of your own consciousness, you can respond to life's challenges with greater wisdom.

Why Not All Prayers Are Answered?

Many people imagine a great superpower in the sky who will one day solve their problems. But nature doesn't work through wishful thinking — it works through laws.

At the deepest level, the universe is built from tiny particles — atoms, molecules, quarks, and waves of subtle energy. Your inner energy must align with the universal energy for your prayers or intentions to bear fruit. That's why only sincere, heart-felt prayers often work — because they naturally tune you to that universal frequency.

Stepping Stone

Meditation acts like a bridge, it connects your inner self with the greater flow of the universe. When you sit quietly, the noise inside begins to fade, and you can start noticing the finer layers of your thoughts and feelings. This practice helps your energy fall in tune with the natural rhythm of life.

When your heartbeat matches nature's beat, life no longer feels like a daily struggle. Instead of swimming against the current, you learn to flow with it. This makes you calmer during tough times and also unlocks a hidden strength within you—one that helps you create, achieve, and inspire in ways you may have never thought possible.

CHAPTER 8

UNDERSTANDING THE MIND & ITS POTENTIAL

The powerhouse of miracles lies within you

What is the Mind, Really?

Many assume the brain and the mind are identical, yet they are not—the two are different in nature. The brain has a physical form. The mind is subtle, intangible, and spread throughout your body.

The brain sits in your skull, a biological control center, but the mind permeates every cell. Every cell in the body holds its own unique memory imprint.. The itch on your arm or the sudden warmth in your chest isn't just a random nerve reaction—it's your cell memory responding. The brain processes and stores these sensations, but the mind is the field in which they arise.

This becomes clearer when you consider life forms with no brain—corals, jellyfish, or trees. They respond, adapt, and even "remember" environmental changes without a brain. Clearly, the mind is not the brain—it is a living presence within and around us.

Conditioning of the Mind & Habit Formation

We perceive the world through five gateways—touch, sight, hearing, smell, and taste. These senses receive stimuli from the world. Our reaction to a stimulus gives birth to thoughts, which in turn give rise to consciousness.

When the same emotions are repeated over and over, they carve grooves in the mind like water etching pathways in stone. These grooves become conditioning patterns that turn into habits. The hopeful truth is that we are not prisoners of these grooves; with awareness, we can redirect the flow and shape new pathways. We have the power to break this cycle. By controlling our reaction to the stimuli, we can break conditioning and recondition the mind.

Example;

Three students are studying together. Music starts playing in the distance.

- One student smiles—it reminds him of a happy childhood memory.
- Another frowns—he finds it distracting.
- The third remains neutral—it doesn't bother him at all.

The stimulus was the same, but the response was different. That's the key: while we can't control external stimuli, we can choose our internal response. Emotions are like fire—reaction is the fuel. Feed a fire of negativity, and it burns stronger. Withdraw the fuel, and it fades. The way we react or otherwise leads to habit formation and our personality is shaped accordingly.

For a detailed understanding, refer to the author's other life-changing book 'The Power of Metta & Mindfulness Meditation.'

Why Is It So Hard to Control Thoughts?

Your brain contains around 86 billion neurons with trillions of connections. Thoughts are electrical signals traveling across these networks. Every time you think a thought—especially with emotion—you strengthen those neural connections. This is why breaking old thought patterns feels like swimming upstream.

The brain acts as a "magnet" for repetition. Feed it fear often, and fear becomes its default. Feed it hope, gratitude, and clarity, and it will slowly rewire itself toward them. This is both the challenge and the opportunity—the mind can be trained, and miracles begin when you consciously magnetize it with what you want.

The Mind's Negative Bias

Our ancestors lived in forests, surrounded by danger. To survive, their minds evolved to constantly scan for threats. That ancient alert system still lives in us today, causing the mind to gravitate toward fear, suspicion, and negativity.

This is why anger, worry, and criticism take root easily, while peace, joy, and gratitude require intentional cultivation.

Emotions as Seeds of Karma

Every emotion you generate is a seed you plant. Some lie dormant in the subconscious, others grow immediately into thoughts, words, and actions—shaping your future.

Because the mind is spread throughout the body, intense negative emotions don't just disturb mental peace—they manifest physically, contributing to stress-related illnesses and even chronic disease.

Synchronizing with Nature

As we learnt, our non-synchronisation and not being in tune with nature causes us to search for truth in the wrong place. We stay confused and distracted. Surrender yourself to the almighty nature, and the answers will begin to appear; the suffering will end. We are not separate from nature—we are threads in its great web.

How to Attune With Nature?

Gratitude is the simplest, most powerful way to align the mind with the rhythms of life. When we harm nature, we harm ourselves. When we honor it through gratitude, we heal ourselves.

The Gardener's Secret

A young man once visited a master gardener known for growing flowers of unmatched beauty. He asked, "What is your secret?"

The gardener smiled, "I pull weeds every day—not because they are bad, but because if I let them grow, they will overtake the flowers. The soil will always grow something. My choice is to decide what thrives."

The master paused for a moment and said, "Think of your mind as fertile soil—whatever seeds you plant will take root and grow." If you don't consciously plant gratitude, peace, and love, weeds of fear and anger will take over. The soil doesn't care—it will grow whatever you feed it."

In Essence:

- Your mind is vast, subtle, and spread throughout your being.
- Conditioning is formed by repeated emotional reactions, but can be rewired.

Thoughts are hard to control because the brain is wired for repetition—use this for your benefit.

- The mind's default bias is negative: positive thinking needs cultivation.
- Your emotions shape your health, your future, and your connection to life.
- Being in tune with nature is the same as being in tune with your own true self.

When you master the gardener's art within, the powerhouse of miracles within you comes alive.

Exercise – Training the Inner Gardener

1. Pause & Scan

Close your eyes and take three slow breaths. Slowly let your awareness travel through your body, like sunlight gently sweeping from the crown of your head down to the tips of your toes. Notice any areas that frequently feel tense, heavy, or restless—these are often where your mind's "weeds" have taken root.

2. Identify the Seed

Ask yourself:

What emotion is strongest in me right now?

When did I first feel it today?

3. Choose Your Crop

Now decide—what emotion would you rather grow instead? Gratitude? Peace? Joy? As you notice different sensations, choose one and immerse yourself in it fully, like holding a single flower and inhaling its fragrance until it fills your being. Initially, it may not be easy to replace the emotion, especially if it is strong. Keep practicing daily, and things will begin to change.

4. Daily Tending

For the next 7 days, repeat this quick check-in once a day. Each time, notice if your "garden" feels clearer and more alive.

Reminder: The soil of the mind will grow whatever you plant. Choose wisely.

CHAPTER 9

THE FIVE-STEP FORMULA

If you wish to find secrets of the Universe, think of energy, frequency, and vibration

– Nikola Tesla

Miracles are happening every moment; we are just ignorant about them. Blooming of a flower, trees dancing to the tune of winds, life-sustaining presence of the sun and the moon, rhythmic beating of our heart, innocent smile of a child, the self-less love of our parents and the pet dog--- so many things are happening around to wake us up from our self-imposed slumber and to make us feel blessed and joyous. Yet, despite all this richness, we often overlook the generosity of nature. Because it gives freely and abundantly, we assume it will always be there, forgetting to treasure its endless gifts. Visualize a day when the sun suddenly disappears, or you open the taps, and there is no water because all the water in this world has evaporated. At that moment, we will realise the importance of the natural resources around us.

Have you ever looked out at the morning sun to thank it for nurturing your life? Have you ever expressed your gratitude toward water while drinking it? How many times do we express our gratitude toward existence and its divinity? And more importantly, have you ever expressed your gratitude toward the divine life energy that exists within you?

Our forefathers were more in tune with nature and always showed gratitude toward nature by celebrating various festivals associated with nature and seasons. Nowadays, the festivals are more about false rituals, dogmas, and superstitions. We have forgotten to respect the significance of nature, the trees, the birds, the stars, and the rivers; there is a systematic rhythm in their existence that we fail to understand. The trees are in synchronization with nature; they produce more fruit than is required. The trees could have managed to reproduce their next generation by producing fewer fruits & seeds; however, they produce in excess to satisfy the needs of living beings. Look at the oceans, from where life originated and sustained; look at the skies and the life-nurturing earth, and we will realise that nature is always in a giving mode, whereas we humans are always in a receiving mode, greedy for more than what is required.

Look towards the creative part of the universal energy where things are being created. The same energy is within and outside us; it wants us to move and be creative, be positively creative towards self and others, be more generous towards others, and be a giver. The difference is that the outside energy is free and moving, while the energy within us has got stuck: it is limited, and the one thing that limits it is our mind. The same mind can be programmed for exploring the immense potential of universal energy, which lies within us.

How to open up this energy and utilize its immense potential for unbelievable success and happiness?

Ingredients That Nurture Positivity

Get ready to understand the five life-changing deeds one needs to follow to alter his or her destiny. Each one of these five ingredients is crucial for nurturing the seed of positivity within ourselves. Though you might have read or heard about them, following them will help you open up and receive blessings from existence. The ingredients are as follows;

1) Gratitude
2) Compassion
3) Charity
4) Wisdom
5) Meditation

Though they appear dull and old-fashioned in today's world, they were and will remain our main tools for a successful and fulfilling life. So read on to understand their extraordinary role in our lives. All five life-changing ingredients are covered one by one in the upcoming chapters.

Closing Remark – Awakening the Inner Energy

Life is never lacking in miracles; what is often missing is our ability to notice them. The five ingredients you are about to explore—**Gratitude, Compassion, Charity, Wisdom, and Meditation**—are not just age-old virtues, but living keys that unlock the immense universal energy within you. They are the bridges between the ordinary and the extraordinary, between surviving and truly living.

When practiced with sincerity, these steps do more than shape your destiny; they tune your energy to the rhythm of the universe. Just as the sun gives without asking, the river flows without stopping, and the tree bears fruit without expecting—so too can you become a channel of positivity, abundance, and joy.

As you move forward into the coming chapters, remember this truth: **you already hold the same creative force that sustains the cosmos.** These five practices will simply help you awaken it, nurture it, and allow it to shine in every aspect of your life.

CHAPTER 10

GRATITUDE

Being grateful for the existence

You are the one you would be talking to the most in your head, so be kind to yourself in your thoughts.

The quality of tomorrow is shaped by how we live today, and today itself is colored by the mindset we awaken with each morning. The state of our mind at dawn quietly sets the tone for the hours ahead. After all, a single day is nothing more than a chain of interconnected moments woven together. Try to start this sequence with positive thoughts before getting out of bed in the morning. The 'good day' or 'bad day' syndrome results from the mind set that we carry. If we wake up in an upset mood, we unknowingly set in motion the sequence of bad events for that day. As you wake up in the morning, the first thing to do is to thank the life energy for your existence and make this a habit. Whatever your mood may be on the previous night, always make it a habit to wake up with gratitude towards the life energy and existence. Before getting down from the bed, just close your eyes and say with sincerity, "Thank you! To the existence of this blessed and beautiful life."

How to Attune With Nature?- Infusing Gratitude into Daily Acts

Gratitude does not wait for grand occasions; it quietly blossoms in life's simplest acts. When you drink water, imagine it as liquid vitality flowing into you. As the glass fills, see it glowing with light; as you sip, sense that light nourishing every cell of your being.

While drinking water, imagine you are drinking liquid life-energy. As you fill your glass, envision it being infused with divine light.

While bathing, place your palms under the water and imagine it washing away not just dust but also tiredness, negativity, and stress, replacing them with blessings and vitality.

While eating, thank the soil, the sun, the rain, the farmers, and the unseen network of life that brought this nourishment to your plate.

Do this often enough and gratitude will no longer be something you practice—it will be something you live.

You are free to create your own unique way of giving thanks and connecting with the infinite energy of the universe. Gratitude can be shown towards the food you eat, the sun, the skies, plants, or living beings. We have become so engrossed in our lives that we have stopped paying attention to nature.

We often forget to notice the silent miracles around us. Yet nature never stops offering them.

Embrace Nature

Do you remember the instances when you were lying or sitting in an open space or garden, and your attention was drawn to the sky? The blue skies and the birds suddenly stopped your thoughts, and calmness prevailed. You experienced the same feeling while visiting your building terrace after a long time and observing the night sky with glittering stars. We have many such memories when the connectedness with nature had a calming effect. Think about your stroll beside the morning sea with the breeze caressing your outer and inner self, or recall the instance while travelling in a streamer with nothing but the vast skies above and blue water below as part of your existence.

Water, sky, sunlight, trees—these are not just elements; they are divine expressions of life itself. When you recognize their sacredness and feel grateful for them, something inside you opens. In doing so, you transform yourself into an open vessel—ready to receive abundance, grace, and blessings.

The Whisper of Gratitude

Gratitude asks for no price, yet it is the richest treasure a human heart can hold. It is the key that unlocks joy without conditions, love without limits, and peace without price.

In the end, gratitude is not just about saying "thank you."

It is about living in such a way that your very presence becomes a silent hymn of appreciation—

It is a quiet offering to life itself, to the vastness of nature, and to the miracle of simply existing in this moment..

Gratitude is the only free thing that brings you the most rewards.

Gratitude is not a word,
It is a light that quietly glows in the heart.
It is the pause between two breaths,
The smile that appears without reason,
The soft thank you to the night sky,
The unseen bridge that connects your inner self with the infinite universe.
When you live with gratitude,
You no longer chase abundance—
Abundance chases you.

So, let every step you take
Be a thankful to the earth beneath your feet,
Let every glance at the sky
And let every heartbeat
Be a thank you to life…
For allowing you to be here,
In this one, precious moment.

CHAPTER 11

THE MAGIC OF COMPASSION

You are the first victim of your negativity- S.N.Goenka

Noted physicist Stephen Hawking had predicted that we humans have only 100 more years of life on earth. Climate change and fast-paced technological advances will probably be responsible for this to happen.

This is also because we have more engineers, doctors, scientists, and industrialists among us than humans.

The basis of being a human is compassion towards other fellow beings and all life forms. Our planet desperately needs many more of them if we have to survive longer. Not just for survival but for harmonious coexistence, we need to be compassionate.

The world is suffering because we fail to understand that being happy is a collective process. Sharing love and kindness is the only way to make ourselves and others happy. We are a byproduct of society and the circumstances surrounding us..

Happiness --- Collective Influence of Society

Our behaviour, our happiness are directly related to the society we live in. The way we dress, eat or behave is the combined outcome of society. A person staying alone in a forest will not bother about his dressing style as nobody is around to notice. Society influences us to behave in a particular way. We have lost our natural way of living and started mimicking the ways of society. Since people around us are rushing around, we too unknowingly behave in the same manner, carrying the crowd mentality. This has given rise to emotional as well as physical ailments. Nobody around us seems happy. Since our unhappiness is a combined outcome of mass behaviour, the whole fabric of society suffers. Though a person in India may think that the cutting of forests in the faraway Amazon is irrelevant to him, in the long run, he is bound to suffer due to climate change and the disasters that will follow. We remain ignorant about the outcome since the effect is not immediately visible and is felt over time. The coronavirus pandemic that shook the whole world in recent times is an example of our greatest responsibility to work collectively for co-existence.

Please understand that when there is a disturbance in any part of the universe, its effect is felt on the whole of the universe. A dying star several light-years away explodes and affects the entire universe. Let's take the example of our own body; if any part of the body gets hurt, then our whole self becomes restless. Thus, if people around us are unhappy, then their negative vibe is bound to affect us as we are part of this single body of existence. The larger the number of unhappy people larger will be its effect on us. This is the reason for the world's suffering, as we lack compassion towards each other.

Importance of Compassionate Co-existence

There is an abundance of everything to satisfy mankind's needs, but the uneven distribution of resources due to greed is causing humankind to suffer. Looking around, we will notice that the world is unhappy, the nations are unhappy, the community is unhappy, the family is unhappy- no wonder you too are unhappy. When everyone around you is unhappy, you too will carry the same vibe, as we all are universally interconnected. So, what's the solution? Compassion towards each other is the only solution.

Start practising compassion, and your life will start changing. This is because compassion starts purifying your inner self, and as learned earlier, nature rewards the person who purifies himself. So, at least for your own sake, start practising compassion.

Our interconnection with others can be further understood by considering the example of a necklace made up of colourful beads. Though the beads may look different because of their shapes, sizes, and colours, the underlying thread that passes through them to form the necklace is the same. Similarly, the thread of cosmic energy woven through all of us is the same. You are as connected to me as with a tribal living deep down in an African forest. And since we all are interconnected, the compassion generated by you will firstly benefit you before passing on to the other living being. This is the reason that compassionate people experience more happiness, abundance and success.

Once we understand this interconnection, there would be no hatred or jealousy, and we would see the other person as a reflection of our own. By helping others, we indirectly help ourselves. Take the example of a share market where your progress depends on the investment made by others in the same stock as yours. As they make a fortune, you feel happy because your fortune is interlinked with theirs. Similarly, we share the same air, skies, resources, and planet. Our progress and happiness are interdependent on others. A person with abundant wealth and luxuries cannot enjoy it if he is living in a war-torn region or surrounded by people living in extreme poverty, as he will always live in fear of his wealth being targeted by the needy.

How to develop compassion?

Compassion is nothing but our ability to love others unconditionally. We do not need to develop compassion; it is already inbuilt into our system. We only need to remove the debris of conditioning from within to allow the stream to flow. It is therefore important to check our love quotient first by sincerely answering the following question;

Name the person whom you curse or blame the most in your life?

Take your time to recollect the name of that one person who makes you feel angry or disappointed. Also, recollect moments of your emotional outburst against that person.

You might have recollected a few names. But in actuality, you may have missed the real name. Well, in most cases, the one person whom you curse or blame the most is yourself.

We go on cursing ourselves without knowing the effect of such outbursts on our lives. We go on blaming or talking ill of ourselves by repeatedly saying, I'm stupid, I'm a failure, my mind has stopped working, I'm unlucky, etc.

These unwarranted comments unknowingly influence our minds; the more we repeat them, the more we repeat them, the greater their effect on our minds and inner selves. As told earlier, the mind has no mind of its own and believes in everything you feed into it with emotions.

So, who needs your compassion the most? It is you who needs your compassion first. If the heart cannot embrace itself with love, how can it truly open to embrace another? Loving yourself is the first flame; only then can its light be shared with the world. The first step is, therefore, to stop feeding negative comments about yourself into your mind. Your thoughts would be directed primarily at you, so be kind to yourself.

Compassion melts negativity. With this positive energy, passion flourishes, and it becomes easy to reach your goal.

Method to develop compassion

Love and compassion are our basic nature. It lies in our core. However, our mentality to find fault and blame others has overshadowed our compassionate nature, and it may therefore be challenging to be compassionate initially. Practice is the only way. Prayer and expressing goodwill towards others are the best way to develop compassion, but do remember not to involve any god or religious figure in your prayers of compassion. This is because your prayer should be a direct one-to-one connection with the person. Involving a god or a religious figure diverts your inner divine energy towards the god instead of the person. Your compassion should be natural, free-flowing between you and the receiver, with no third party involved. This way, your mind will realise the strength of the divine energy lying within your body, thereby strengthening it. There are situations when our mind naturally tends to show compassion; visiting a hospital and being subjected to the plight of patients suffering due to various ailments, seeing a funeral, and hearing the heart-wrenching cries of the young child who has lost his mother, may bring out the compassion from within. We need not wait for such unfortunate incidents for our compassion to arise. We need to develop an ability to express compassion in normal situations, too. It is possible to be compassionate in all kinds of good or bad situations.

Example:

1) Once, while visiting a hospital, I saw a burn patient being treated for his wounds, The screams that followed reminded me of our helplessness in such a situation. However, what I did in my mind was to pray compassionately and wholeheartedly for his recovery and wish him the strength to cope with the situation. He was unknown to me, but his plight moved my inner self to pray and show compassion towards him. My prayers were directly channeled to

him, thereby cleansing my inner self. If instead, I had prayed to god, then I would have left it to god to help him, thereby missing the opportunity to involve and empower my inner self.

2) In our day-to-day life, as we walk down the street, we may come across a beggar or a mentally disturbed person. We may or may not be in a position to help them, but we can at least wholeheartedly show compassion by wishing good for them in our minds.
3) Visiting a marriage ceremony and seeing the happy smiling couple, don't just outwardly and artificially wish them. Involve your inner self to wish them good wholeheartedly. Also, wish them good in your mind a few more times during the ceremony.
4) While watering the plants on your balcony, you may gently touch them and wholeheartedly wish them a long, healthy, and blooming life.

These are just a few examples, and you can self-create your compassionate moments in day-to-day life.

Challenges

Agreed, it may not always be possible for you to be sincere in offering your compassion. It may feel forced, but still wish others good with whatever level of sincerity you can offer. Practice will eventually increase the honesty of your wishes. Your inner self will begin to change, thereby becoming more receptive to receiving blessings and goodwill from the universe. Whatever you give, you receive back!.

There is no need to follow any particular ritual or elaborate prayer to do so. Just say in your mind, 'bless you, dear'. As you practice, you will notice that the faith factor within you increases. This increase in faith will help you to deal with your problems.

We can also show compassion at the time of happiness or in any other situation. The more compassion you show towards others, the more positive energy you will be drawing within yourself.

Gratitude and compassion work like a soap that removes stains of negativity from our inner self.

CHAPTER 12

THE POWER OF CHARITY

Giving is the most receptive of all acts. We give from the finite, but we receive from the infinite

– Putnam

What is charity? Well, this appears to be a silly question. We all know what precisely a charity is, or at least we think we know about it. Once you go through this chapter, you will realise that charity (called dana in India) has a deeper perspective. Most of us are not aware that charity can be classified into different types. Go through the following types to know your charitable nature.

Self-convenient charity

Most of the things that we do as a charity are nothing but getting rid of unwanted items. Giving leftover food to a beggar or a dog, giving old, not in use clothes to poor children, is what we think charity is. Well, of course, it qualifies as charity, wherein you are at least not throwing away the leftover food or clothes and reaching out to someone who needs it. This also carries merit and will eventually get some good karma/deeds to your credit. But this type of Dana is ordinary because you gave the things only because you no longer needed them. Here, you are not making any extra effort, and giving away was a convenient way out. Even helping others with the desire to gain something in return falls in this category.

Reaching out to someone

Here in this type of charity, you make efforts to help others. Arranging food for the people during the pandemic, organizing medical camps for the needy, etc., can be considered under this category.

The superior charity (Maha Dana)

This is instantaneous and selfless charity, wherein the compassion within you stirs your inner self to go ahead and do something beyond the ordinary.

The Story of Superior Charity

Long ago, a wanderer set out from his small village on a journey toward a faraway town. He started early in the morning and reached the outskirts of the town by afternoon. Being poor, he had limited food, had not eaten anything since morning, and was hungry due to the long travel. He spotted a large tree and sat underneath its cool shadow to have his meal. He untied the piece of cloth within which the food was kept. He had a bhakri (roti or flat round bread made from millet) and chutney. He was desperate to stuff the meal in his mouth and was just about to take his first morsel when a hungry old man appeared before him and begged for food. The traveller, without giving a second thought, immediately gave half of his bhakri to the poor old man. No hesitation, just a heart full of compassion to understand the desperate condition of that hungry person. This is superior charity (Maha Dana). A person with millions in his bank account and then donating a few thousand to gain the holy grace is not as virtuous as compared to a layman who strives hard towards the upliftment of street children, even with his limited economic resources.

I have nothing to offer in charity (excuse)

Charity does not involve just giving money or goods. A compassionate person will find a way to help others even in the absence of riches. Hence, 'I have nothing to offer in charity' is a lame excuse.

Giving your time to attend to the needs of elderly people in your neighbourhood or an old-age home, imparting education to children from a nearby slum, or even giving your shoulder to someone to cry upon and listening patiently to their grief, qualifies as charity. The only necessity is the urge to be of some use to others.

When you are blessed with plenty,
share your abundance; when you have little,
share your love.

– Rumi

Those who strive wholeheartedly for the service of others receive manifold rewards from nature. If you want to fill in with abundance, then pour it out into charity. Give to receive.

Balancing Greed With Charity

There is nothing wrong in earning money—wealth itself is not sinful. But never let guilt cling to your earnings, nor let your joy be chained to them. Money can meet your needs, yet it cannot buy inner peace or lasting happiness. The more we let money dominate our pursuit, the further we drift from true contentment. Giving to others through acts of kindness and charity restores balance, softening our greed with goodness. Just as nature always seeks harmony, we too must learn the art of balance. Whenever a desire arises, let it be paired with an equal wish to serve and give back to humanity.

Charity is essential, but it is wise to identify genuine people who need it. Charity is from the heart, but we must also keep our minds alert to do it the right way. Here comes the role of wisdom.

Mirror of Truth

Charity is more than an act of generosity—it is a reminder of our shared humanity. It serves as a bridge, carrying support from those who have more to those who are in need. Yet, true charity is not only about giving from the heart; it also requires wisdom. Without wisdom, even the noblest intentions may be misdirected. When we give thoughtfully—ensuring our help reaches the right hands in the right way—our charity becomes a force of real transformation. To give wisely, selflessly, and wholeheartedly is to align ourselves with the very rhythm of nature: balance, compassion, and harmony.

CHAPTER 13

WISDOM

Our guiding light

After reading about Compassion & Charity in the previous chapters, here comes a word of caution. Charity should be done to the deserving and not to the pretender (one who fools us into believing that they need our help). Compassion leads to charity, but compassion should not blind us to reaching out to help just about anybody. Learn to say no to the undeserving one, and that too without feeling guilty about it; otherwise, you may end up sentimental instead of compassionate.

If we are not careful about our charity, then we may end up helping the drunkard who uses our money for his alcohol needs. In India, we see poor, malnourished children begging on the street; giving money to these children will enrich the begging syndicate, which uses them for their selfish means. This will further increase child abuse and trafficking.

Here comes the role of wisdom!

Wisdom is the key, not only in terms of charity but also in our overall decision-making process in life.

Though self-help books hardly talk about wisdom. I believe wisdom is the most significant factor for success and happiness. Cultivating and enhancing wisdom should be our prime goal and other good things will follow, as wisdom helps us at every stage of life. Wisdom is more important than knowledge. Wisdom is superior to intelligence.

Being Practical is the key.

As wisdom grows, we realise that being compassionate doesn't mean being emotional or oversensitive. I realised this the hard way through my experiences with different people in my life. Since I was always ready to help and felt it difficult to say 'No' to the people who approached me for monetary help. I ended up helping most of them. Most of them never bothered to return the money, and I convinced myself with the feeling of satisfaction to not bother, as helping others is a noble deed. But gradually, I realised my mistake of helping even the undeserving ones. Some so-called acquaintances suffered financial problems due to their own wrongdoings, and I ended up helping them. They never took efforts to correct their financial situation and thereby I decided to never help them again financially. I learned to say 'No'.

After all, it was my hard-earned money; I was putting lots of sweat, effort and time to earn it. Why should it be given to the people who do not care about improving their situation or respecting my money?

Most of the time, due to fear of losing a person, we burden ourselves with unwanted people in our lives. There are friends who, after little or no contact over the years, suddenly appear one fine morning for financial help, you fall for their sob story, and end up helping them. Later, you learn about the habitual practice of that person to contact old acquaintances (through social media, it is easy now) and ask for money.

This is my personal experience that such a type of person who was hardly in touch with you over the years will again disappear into the no-contact zone. Hence, keeping such people at bay is advisable. You have limitations and cannot help everyone by falling prey to their emotional stories.

So, what is the lesson?

Avoid or limit financial help to those who are themselves responsible for their problems and are not ready to work on improving their situation.

Learn to understand people. If a friend or acquaintance is just an opportunist and needs financial assistance, then you may help them with the condition of returning the money within a certain time period. If they forget to fulfill their word, do not hesitate to gently remind them of the promise they made. That way, he will at least not turn to you for help the next time. If they don't appreciate the efforts you put in to earn your money, then you too needn't respond to them.

There are some exceptions, though. During the COVID pandemic, some individuals actually required assistance, and I didn't hesitate to offer it to them to the best of my abilities.

It is our moral responsibility to help. But it is also a matter of wisdom to identify the people who deserve the help.

Here we are talking only about financial help. Definitely, we have to help our closest family members, dear ones and close friends as per our capability without any expectations in return. This is the investment we need to make in our close relationships. Some relationships cannot be valued in money.

We can also help in many other ways, like making ourselves available during their hour of need.

This was all about 'help', where we need to be cautious while making financial decisions.

Clarity About Charity

Now, let's talk about charity. In charity, there is no question of expecting anything in return. Helping the orphans in an orphanage or providing assistance to the old people in old age homes are examples of charity: it is our social responsibility, and we should not shy away from it.

I knew the power of charity, but for a major part of my life mixed it up with the concept of help. Most of us have gone through the experiences discussed above, and hence, before you help someone understand the difference between Help & Charity. This will save you from lots of heartache and losses over the years.

As elaborated above, CHARITY & HELP are two different things;

Charity is a help, but help is not always charity.

Charity is compulsory, but help is optional.

Wisdom is therefore very important in the overall decision-making process, not just limited to charity.

Wisdom is therefore very important in the overall decision-making process not just limited to charity.

Meditation enhances wisdom and helps us to differentiate between right and wrong. As you go deeper into the inner core of yourself through meditation, the laws of nature that govern our inner and outer world are revealed. You no longer depend on scriptures for guidance as your inner light burns bright. Wisdom is the wick of that light. The Buddha's words, 'Be a light unto yourself,' hold the truth.

Pearl of Wisdom

Unlike the four components, i.e., Gratitude, compassion, charity, and meditation; wisdom cannot be practised. Wisdom needs to be developed. It is the by-product of meditation. Once we start to practice meditation, wisdom follows and, in turn, strengthens meditation. Meditation and wisdom are complementary to each other and act as a supplement for enhancing one another.

Basics of Meditation

Due to our limited knowledge about meditation, we wrongly associate meditation with silencing of mind. In truth, meditation is not about forcing thoughts to stop or controlling them with effort. Instead, it is about cultivating a calm awareness—watching whatever arises without judgment, without attachment, and without resistance.

Meditation is not confined to the mind alone; it embraces body, action, and speech as well. A restless mind unsettles the body, just as bodily imbalance can disturb the mind. In the same way, our thoughts are closely tied to speech, for thoughts are simply the mind speaking (mind talk) within.

For this reason, meditation is far more than the mere quieting of the mind—it is a practice of harmonizing mind, body, and speech through non-reactive awareness.

For more than 50 Meditation Techniques, refer to the author's other book 'Meditation on the go-Meditate anywhere, anytime'

CHAPTER 14

MEDITATION

To the mind that is still, the whole universe surrenders

– Lao Tzu

Basics of Meditation

Understanding the foundation before stepping into practice When we hear the word meditation, many of us immediately picture someone sitting cross-legged with eyes closed, lost in silence. Because of this limited view, we often assume that meditation means "stopping the mind" or "forcing thoughts to disappear." But this is not true.

Meditation is not about suppression or forceful control of the mind. Rather, it is about cultivating awareness—a gentle, non-reactive observation of whatever arises, without judgment, attachment, or aversion. It is about creating inner balance, so that thoughts, emotions, and sensations can be witnessed with clarity instead of being fought against.

More importantly, meditation is not just a mental activity. It is deeply connected to the body and speech as well. A troubled mind unsettles the body; and a restless body, in turn keeps the mind from finding ease. Similarly, our thoughts are closely tied to our speech, because thoughts are nothing but subtle "mind-talk."

This is why true meditation is a practice of bringing silence to three interconnected levels of being:

- Silence of Body
- Silence of Speech
- Silence of Mind

Let us understand each of these in detail.

1. Silence of Body

If the body is restless, the mind cannot remain calm. Our posture, gestures, and even unconscious movements mirror our state of mind.

For example, you may have noticed people sitting on a chair, constantly shaking their legs, or twisting their posture. This is the body's subtle way of releasing inner anxiety. While it seems harmless, it shows how inner turbulence immediately spills into physical movement.

Interestingly, our hands often want to quiver too, but since it is socially inappropriate to keep shaking hands in public, the legs become the outlet of mental restlessness.

This is why meditation begins with stabilizing the body. In most traditions, you are asked to sit in a posture where the limbs are placed in a steady, balanced way—often with crossed legs, a straight spine, and hands resting gently. The posture is not just symbolic; it "locks" the body and reduces unnecessary movement.

A still body becomes a foundation for a still mind. That is why the silence of the body is considered the first gateway to meditation.

2. Silence of Speech

What exactly is a thought? In essence, it is nothing but the silent chatter of the mind.

On deeper observation, you will notice something remarkable: many thoughts are subtly accompanied by a tiny movement of the tongue or throat muscles, even though you are not speaking out loud. This shows the intimate link between speech and thinking.

This is why in traditional meditation retreats, such as Vipassana, practitioners are asked to observe noble silence for several days. By refraining from speaking, the mind's habit of producing endless words and conversations begins to slow down.

The silence of speech is not just about avoiding sound—it is about reducing the traffic of unnecessary thoughts.

As external chatter fades, inner chatter also gradually weakens.

3. Silence of Mind

Finally, we arrive at the most profound level—the silence of the mind.

This is not achieved by forcefully stopping thoughts but by learning to observe them with awareness. When we stop reacting—neither chasing pleasant thoughts nor resisting unpleasant ones—the mind slowly settles on its own.

Just as muddy water clears when left undisturbed, the mind too becomes naturally transparent and peaceful when we allow it to rest in silence.

One-Minute Guided Meditation: The Three Silences

Sit comfortably with your spine upright, steady yet relaxed—not rigid.. Gently close your eyes.

Step 1 – Silence of Body

Bring awareness to your body. Notice if your hands, legs, or shoulders are moving restlessly. Gently allow them to become still. Imagine your body as a calm mountain, steady and grounded.

Step 2 – Silence of Speech

Now, bring attention to your lips and tongue. Let them relax completely. Feel the sweetness of silence, as though every word has melted away. No need to speak—outside or inside. Let silence be your language.

Step 3 – Silence of Mind

Gently bring your attention to your thoughts. See them rise and fade like passing clouds in the open sky. There is no need to chase them or push them away—simply observe and allow them to dissolve. Beyond those clouds, the boundless sky of pure awareness is always present.

Take one deep, slow breath in… and breathe out gently.

For this one minute, you are whole, you are still, and you are free.

CHAPTER 15

MEDITATION MADE SIMPLE: PRACTICES FOR DAILY LIFE

The best way to take care of the future is to take care of the present moment.

– Thích Nhất Hạnh

This chapter introduces simple meditation techniques that help cultivate this state of inner silence. But always remember: the foundation lies in the harmony of body, speech, and mind.

Achievements and happiness are dependent upon how focused you are. Focus is dependent upon your level of consciousness at any given moment. Meditation improves focus, thereby improving overall well-being.

How many thoughts are there in your mind at this moment?

Even while you are reading this, your mind frequently wavers in some other direction. The mind is not entirely focused on the task at hand. The clouds of thoughts create a haze in our minds and cause difficulty in decision-making. This, in turn, gives rise to stress and anxiety. Trying hard to focus on work or to get rid of stress and anxiety further worsens the situation. The harder we try, the more difficult it becomes.

I remember one of these experiences during my engineering days. During one of the exams, the answer to one particular question was known to me. But suddenly, I went blank. I tried hard to recollect, but the answer had vanished from my mind. In the evening, while relaxing, the answer suddenly popped up in my mind without any effort. This happens to almost everyone of us at some point in time. This example shows the importance of a relaxed, uncluttered mind for accessing the answer. This happens to almost every one of us at some point in time. This example shows the importance of a relaxed un-cluttered mind for accessing the answer.

The reflection of the moon in a pool of water will be visible to us only when we allow the water to calm down. The moon's reflection is always there. We are just unable to see it due to ripples in the water. The same is true about the truth or answers within us. The truth is always there to be fetched, but our disturbed mind makes it difficult to access the same.

Further, once the mind is conditioned through meditation, it brings about a significant change in our lifestyle. Positivity, success, peace, and tranquillity are all related to our state of mind. Psychologists say that depression and sadness are sometimes due to how we relate to the past, while anxiety is due to our anticipation of the future.

Most of us associate meditation with some kind of mysterious process. Some think it is difficult. At the same time, others think that meditation can be done only by sitting in a particular pose and keeping the eyes closed. Meditation is a way to deal with your thinking and reacting process. You can self-create your techniques by observing the way the mind reacts to certain situations.

For example, every morning, I have developed a habit of observing the garden and trees outside my balcony. The greenery and the cool breeze make my thoughts disappear for some time. We all have experienced situations when our mind goes into a trance-like state; that is nothing but a glimpse of our meditative state.

In this book, we will discuss some very basic mind training techniques only. A higher level of meditation requires time, commitment, and proper training, and hence is not dealt with here. Some of the simple mind training techniques are given below for different situations.

For workplace anxiety

Grounding Technique

Let's first understand that there exists a correlation between our body and mind. When our mind is stressed, the body by default gets stressed, and since it is difficult to control the mind, we will try to control our physical movements to relieve the anxiety.

When the mind is disturbed, we can easily feel the stress and anxiety occupying it, but we fail to see its simultaneous effect on the body. Relaxing the untrained mind in such a situation is difficult, but relaxing the body is comparatively easy. Hence, we will try to relax the body instead of the mind, and consequently, the mind also gets relaxed to a certain extent. For example, you are sitting in your office and trying to finish the work before the deadline. The mind is running fast. What reaction does your body exhibit? Pause a little and pay attention to your body. If you are sitting, then the first thing you would notice is that either the sole of your feet is not touching the ground, you are twisting your ankle, or you are shaking your legs. In short, your legs are restless. Though this appears to be a regular habit, this is nothing but mental stress on the body. Your legs are thus mimicking your mental state. Now, consciously put your foot in an ordinary ground-touching situation (the soles completely touching the ground) and stop any type of leg movements. Don't try hard; just allow the legs to relax in that position, and some part of your mental stress will be gone. Make it a habit to observe your leg's behaviour in normal situations too, and consciously bring it in contact with the ground, thereby grounding yourself. Next, imagine the remaining mental stress passing through your body into the ground and Mother Nature taking care of it. This hardly takes any time, and the benefit you gain is much more than the time spent on this activity. Your performance will be enhanced, and the chances of errors reduced.

For stress reduction

Observing Your Thoughts

In this meditation technique, sit quietly and close your eyes. Observe the arising and passing away of your thoughts without being judgmental about them. The thought could be daily routine related or may contain moments of happiness or sorrow. Just observe them without reacting; no aversive reaction towards painful thoughts or attachment towards joyful thoughts. Remaining equanimous is the key. Try this for five minutes initially. Increase the duration gradually over the days.

For relaxation

This technique can be used for all routine situations in our day-to-day life. This technique is also helpful if you are about to face an exam or an interview the next day.

Conscious Listening

Sit comfortably, close your eyes, and notice the sounds around you, starting with the first one you hear. Listen for 1-2 minutes (approximately). It may be the sound of a fan or the sound of wind chimes. Next, move your attention to the next sound within the room, don't try hard, and again stay with that sound for 1-2 minutes. Continue till you don't find any sound in the room. Next, take your mental attention outside that room and listen to outdoor sounds near your house. You may hear the chirping of a bird, the sounds of children playing, etc. Stay with individual sounds for a few minutes. Next, move your attention towards sound from a distant place; this may include a dog barking at some faraway place, sounds of vehicles from the road, etc. Stay with those sounds for a few minutes and then again come back to the first sound you started with, i.e., the sound of the fan, and here the meditation ends. The crux of this technique lies in remaining equanimous and not reacting to whatever you hear. This means not becoming joyous for a pleasant musical sound nor getting irritated by the cawing of a crow.

For grief or trauma

Grief is nothing but a chain of powerful thoughts that overpowers one's mind. This is the most difficult mental state, and coming out of it is very difficult. Though time is required to overcome this state of mind, some relief can be experienced through the following technique.

Division of conscious attention span

Sit in an upright position and close your eyes. Now you will purposely divide your thought span. Since the thoughts in traumatic conditions are never-ending, you now need to make a conscious (but not forceful) effort to divide your thoughts into smaller time spans. Decide that you will not allow any negative or traumatic thoughts to creep into your mind for the next 30 seconds. See if you can succeed. If yes, then continue to not think about any negative, traumatic thought for the next 15 seconds and so on. This way, you are creating a chain of non-traumatic thoughts, and the pattern of the mind for continuously holding on to the chain of traumatic thoughts will be broken. The chain needs to be broken. This is further explained below with an example.

Let's take an example of a person who has recently lost his job and cannot overcome the grief. He will need to make a conscious, determined effort not to allow the thoughts related to his job loss to come to his mind for a specific duration (say 60 seconds) and then keep increasing that duration.

Here, he needs to understand that a disturbed mind will only aggravate his situation and affect his physical and mental health. Hence, trying to divide his attention span as above will help him break the stream of disturbing thoughts and help him find a solution.

This technique can also be applied to our normal day-to-day routine. The only difference is that the attention division span time would be a little longer than that in a traumatic condition. You may do this for 5 minutes and decide that, whatever your problems, you would not allow any negative thoughts to occupy your mind for the next 5 minutes. This can be done at any time. While cooking or doing your laundry, just decide and make a determined effort not to allow any problem-related thoughts to enter your mind for that period. You may find it difficult initially, but if practised regularly, you will create a chain of such problem-free thought spans in your mind. Remember, the mind can overcome a problem or find a solution only when it gets some time to break away from the situation. This technique helps to do so.

Do it Right Now

Why not do this exercise right now? Keep this book aside. No need to close your eyes. Just ensure that you are not allowing any negative thoughts to enter your mind for the next 5 minutes. You may do so while sitting, moving around, and while doing some other work. Regularly practise this by gradually increasing the time duration.

The collection of such moments, positive or negative, affects our personality and also our karma. Life is all about a collection of spans stitched together.

Golden Thread

No need to seek far, no need to chase—
Calm already lives in your inner space.
Close your eyes, let the ripples cease,

And taste the quiet river of peace.

As the mind becomes tranquil, wisdom arises, which in turn guides us towards the ultimate truth. This journey begins with the practice of meditation.

CHAPTER 16

WAY TO ATTAIN INNER PEACE

I'm at peace.

I'm at peace with myself.

I'm at peace with my surroundings.

Pause here for a moment.

Read these lines again—slowly, as if you are speaking directly to your own heart. If possible, close your eyes. Speak them softly with trust, and observe—does your body relax? Does your breathing ease, even slightly? Do you feel a gentle breeze of calm touching the edges of your restless mind?

If yes, then you have just experienced a glimpse of how quickly the mind can be reconditioned. A tiny doorway has opened, showing you that peace is not far away, not outside of you, not hidden in distant mountains or in possessions—it is already within you, waiting to be unlocked.

We all long for peace. Yet, in truth, very few live in complete peace. Some carry it like a faint fragrance, some as a passing breeze, and some struggle to feel it at all. Inner calm is not a gift given only to a chosen few—it is a state of mind that can be cultivated and trained, just as a muscle can be strengthened or a garden can be nurtured.

But before we learn the art of peace, we must understand what steals it away from us. Why do we lose our calm so easily? Why does the mind wander into storms of stress, conflict, and unrest?

The answer lies in one root emotion—the Big "F."

Yes, Fear.

The Role of Fear

Fear is the father of anxiety, the mother of stress, and the silent seed of many restless states. If we are asked to point out the most negative human emotion that affects us the most, we can quickly point out anger, jealousy, hatred, greed, etc. But fear is the most crucial factor that we ignore. It wears masks—anger, jealousy, greed, insecurity, hatred—but if you peel away these layers, you'll often find fear sitting silently at the core.

The strange thing is, most of us do not admit our fears. We think acknowledging fear is a sign of weakness or cowardice. So, we pretend to be brave, while inside our hearts may be trembling. By pushing fear under the carpet of our awareness, we give it more power. Hidden fears do not disappear—they grow in the dark, like weeds in an untended garden. One day, they rise up stronger and scarier than ever before.

Fear, however, is not our enemy. It is our most primitive companion, present since the very beginning of life. Fear is embedded in us from our earliest moments of life, unlike anger or jealousy, which develop later through circumstances..

Think of birth itself:

Inside the mother's womb, the baby floats in complete security. All needs are met effortlessly, without struggle. But during birth, the infant experiences a sudden, shocking separation from its safe world. It is thrust into an unknown environment of bright lights, loud sounds, and strange sensations. These unexpected happenings instill a response of fear in the baby. That loud first cry is not just a cry of life—it is also the cry of fear.

This primal emotion once served a crucial purpose. For our ancestors, fear meant survival. It sharpened their senses against predators in the forests, warned them of danger, and guided their decisions. Even today, fear can alert us, protect us, and keep us safe.

But when fear is unchecked—when it takes control instead of guiding—it becomes destructive. It paralyzes the mind, clouds judgment, drains energy, and creates an endless loop of stress and worry.

Three Roots of Fear

Our fears often sprout from three different time zones of life:

1) **The Past**
   Old wounds, past failures, painful memories—our minds replay them and create a lens of doubt through which we see the present.
2) **The Future**
   Anticipation of "what if?"—fear of failure, rejection, or loss—creates anxiety about what has not even happened yet.
3) **The Present**
   Restlessness in the here and now—overthinking, comparing, judging—makes us unable to simply be at peace with the moment.

The mind often drifts between memories of the past and worries about the future, seldom settling in the present moment—and this continual wandering gives rise to fear, anxiety, and inner unrest.

Facing Fear

Being fearless does not mean eliminating fear. To erase fear would be impossible—and unwise, because fear also carries wisdom. True fearlessness means acknowledging the fear.

It means looking in to the fear and whispering to its presence with compassion.

"Yes, I see you. Yes, I feel you. And it's okay."

The moment you acknowledge fear, it loses half its grip. The more you run from it, the bigger the shadow grows. But when you pause, face it, and breathe with it, you find it shrinking into its proper size—just another emotion, not a monster.

Fear is like a child crying in the dark. If you ignore it, the cry grows louder. But if you gently turn toward it, hold it, and reassure it, the crying quiets down.

And when fear is soothed, peace naturally flows in.

Facing the Truth

The best way to handle the fear is to acknowledge and face it. It's ok to accept in your mind that I'm fearful, I'm afraid. If you try to push it beneath the carpet of your mind, then it will keep on lurking there, just like the monster in horror movies. Which not only keeps on haunting regularly but will one day also appear in a more frightening form.

CHAPTER 17

HOW TO DEAL WITH PAST EVENTS?

I follow four dictates Face it, accept it, deal with it, and then let it go

– Sheng Yen

Each of us holds the weight of our past experiences. Though the incident may have ended long ago, it still lives somewhere inside us, quietly shaping our moods, thoughts, and even our health.

Complete the past events

What we need to do is to work to finish such unfinished memories. Go back into your past, and you will find many such memories. Recollect those memories in your mind and work on them. Completing the Past Events.

Certain memories slowly dissolve like fading ripples, while others stay vivid, piercing into our present moment.

Unfinished memories are like open files in the mind—they consume energy until we bring them to completion. To heal, we must revisit them not to dwell, but to finish the unfinished business with compassion.

Real Life Incidence

Let me give one such example from my school days. A schoolmate made mischief in the class, and the teacher thought that I, too, was involved in it. The teacher admonished me in front of the class for no mistake of mine. The school Principal called my parents, and again I felt insulted in front of my classmates. I was severely angry with that teacher, and the memory lingered in my mind for a long. After 20 years, while working on various meditation techniques, I checked whether old memories were still unknowingly affecting me. So, I recollected past problematic memories one after another. When this particular memory came to my mind, I still felt the same kind of negative emotions that were associated with that incident then. I realised that the incident had ended long back and nobody, i.e. schoolmates or my parents, remembers it, nor would that teacher of mine have bothered to remember it. Then why should I allow this memory to linger in my mind? Since the memory is in my mind, I need to counter it in my mind only, not by force or repulsion, but by compassion. I decided to get rid of this memory by closing my eyes, sincerely sending compassion to that teacher, and saying that I have forgiven you and may existence bless you.

Remember, your present nature is constituted from such past events. Once such memories are weakened by facing them compassionately, your nature will begin to change positively. All readers are requested to look back on all such memories that are still hidden in your mind and may be indirectly affecting your present moment. Get rid of those memories. Forgive and forget. If you find it difficult to forgive in the first instance, then try again the next day, and that memory will weaken and fade away eventually.

Events with close relatives & friends

We are more hurt when our close relatives or friends are the reason for such past bad memories.

One of my female clients was struggling with anxiety and depression. Her husband found it difficult to handle her as she was constantly fighting with him by bringing up past events. They were married for more than 40 years, but the lady could not forget the ill-treatment she received at the hands of her in-laws. Right from her initial days of marriage till the following 15 years, she was harassed by her in-laws, due to which her married life suffered. She was made to work even during her pregnancy and was made to eat stale food. Now, even after so many years into marriage, she was still unable to overcome frustration as she thinks that her husband did nothing to help her then. Her in-laws had died way back. But she still curses them daily and holds them responsible for spoiling her prime young married life and causing mental agony. She has grown-up children and has no financial or family issues now. But due to her repeated venting of past events with great intensity, she suffers from physical and mental ailments.

The doctor was treating her for the physical ailments that refused to heal. This was because the Doctor was unaware of the real culprit, i.e., her emotional state, responsible for her physical ailments. Medicines can only cause the symptoms to go away temporarily, but they cannot treat the root cause, which lies in the mind.

I told the lady that it was she, and not her in-laws, who continued to suffer still. I suggested she follow the forgive-and-forget method. It was difficult for her to follow my advice, as cursing the in-laws had become a daily routine, and her mind was hesitant to give up this habit. I then explained to her that by keeping those memories alive, she was indirectly helping her dead in-laws to affect her present and the future. The best way to deal with them was to forgive with compassion and let the law of karma decide the course of action for their behaviour.

Such deep-rooted memories will not go away easily, but at least we can blunt them by sending out compassionate forgiveness. As mentioned earlier, this will not happen in a single day, as the memory has become stronger due to regular remembrance. Hence, repeated compassionate forgiveness over some more days may be required. Aiding this practice with meditation may help further.

Events with unknown people

Often, we find ourselves caught in uneasy or difficult situations with unknown people. This can be an argument with a co-passenger on a train, an argument with a person breaking the queue, etc. The person is unknown, but in the moment of passion, we get into the confrontation mode and lose our patience and peace, and if you are emotional, then the memory of that moment may linger for some time and affect your mood. You may be at fault or otherwise, but since the event has ended and the person was unknown to you, there is no point in allowing that person to linger in your mind. Though not immediately, after the passage of a few hours, if you find that event still affecting you, then either say sorry to that person in your mind(if you realise the fault was yours) or compassionately forgive him and end the event in your mind.

How to Deal with Present Events

Due to our current lifestyle, we quickly become anxious. Being anxious has become our nature. Fear is the cause of our anxiety. We have named this fear as 'Tension', i.e., would I be able to reach the meeting on time? I would miss the deadline? I would miss that train? Etc. This fear doesn't seem to harm us immediately, but that's accumulated bit by bit and leads to other problems in the long term. How to deal with these anxious moments that are happening right now inside me?

Let me again explain this through my own experience. This is related to my daily train commute to the office. I needed to travel by bus or rickshaw to reach the station and then walk through the crowd to catch my train at a particular time. It was an exercise in itself as the bus used to get held up or slowed down due to traffic, and then after alighting, I needed to move through the crowd hurriedly to ensure that the train was not missed. This daily routine created a habit mechanism in me, and soon I realised that even when the bus was not late or the crowd was less, my mind reacted in the same anxious manner, and I used to reach the train with the same feeling of anxiety. Even when I was well in time, I had developed this habit of hurrying myself.

What happens in such a situation? When I hurried to catch the train, I realised that it was not just my body that rushed, but my mind also moved in a hurry. Hurrying the mind is of no use in such a situation, but it happened automatically and caused anxiety. When the body is stressed, the stress reflects on the mind. When we walk hurriedly, the mind also hurries. The same thing happens with most of our activities. Hence, it is essential to pause and remind the mind to allow the body to do the work or it may do more harm than good. The hurrying mind may lead to errors or even accidents. Thus, eventually, I gave auto-suggestions to my mind not to hurry and let the body do all the work. My mindfulness training helped me in dealing with this type of situation.

Go with the Flow Technique

Staying in the present moment with mindful and conscious attention toward the things around us helps us deal with situations. You may be aware or not, but the universe around us is moving, things are constantly changing, and life is happening. Just observe the happenings around. While walking on a busy street, observe the crowd and the traffic moving, and you can feel this movement; we are an inseparable part of this mechanism. We cannot free ourselves from these happenings, and going with the flow will help us attune with life and existence.

This existence is nothing but the play of space and time. Our mind perceives the world as a phenomenon happening in this space at a certain speed of time. We react to the happenings with our senses. Try non-reacting and just observing the happenings, and our perspective towards existence will begin to change.

Just like water in an ocean flows and carries the things within it. Similarly, the existence around us is moving and carrying all of us. While moving in the crowd, just observe the crowd. The people in the crowd and you are nothing but the things moving in this ocean of existence. Life is flowing. The time is flowing. Just try to feel and experience the crowd as flowing. Go with that flow without reacting. Observe the crowd without any judgment or reaction, and the mind will calm down.

Observing the breath (Anapana) technique

This is not an instant method and needs practice. While at home, sit comfortably and close your eyes. Consciously observe the incoming and outgoing flow of the breath. We never notice our breath pattern and therefore remain unaware of its movement. By observation, you will realise that we breathe through either the right or left nostril and sometimes through both. In the beginning, you may not be able to judge the flow of breath; in that case, take a few fast breaths to ascertain the nostril through which it is moving. Then allow the natural flow of breath without any force or judgment. Don't try to control it. Consciously observe the air flow movement through the nostrils. The air is coming in, the air is moving out - should be your focus. Breathing affects our heartbeats; this technique will normalize the heartbeats, and the stress on the mind will be reduced. Once you get hold of this technique, you can use it in any type of day-to-day situation. Initially, you may find it difficult to observe your breath due to thoughts moving across your mind. In that case, as a beginner, you may set a target of observing the first ten breath movements consciously. Go on increasing the count daily till the time comes when you no longer need to count the breath, and observing the breath becomes a natural process.

Practical Example

You're attending a performance review session where the manager is evaluating each employee individually. You are waiting for your turn, but meanwhile, the boss comes down heavily on some of the fellow employees for their below-par performance. Your turn can be anytime soon. You are already anxious due to the lashing of previous employees; the boss looks toward you through his eyeglasses, and your heart is about to skip a beat. After a small pause, the boss continues with his fury and lambasts your performance. He further warns you to achieve a certain target within the remaining days of the week.

Here, there are two situations -

First, you were anxious while waiting your turn, thereby creating tension in your present moment, and second, the bashing and warning from the boss to complete the target within the stipulated time will keep you tense for some time in the future.

In both these situations, you cannot apply the prior techniques, i.e, being compassionate with the boss or going with the flow. Here, the practice of observing the breath may be helpful. As the boss continues to admonish you, just listen to him by attentively observing your breath; this will help you remain in the present moment, thereby not allowing the anxiety to take over you. This technique needs practice and is very helpful in dealing with day-to-day stressful situations.

Live in the Present Moment

Don't just restrict mindful breathing to stressful situations. Make it a part of your daily lifestyle and practice whenever possible i.e. while sitting, walking, and relaxing, before sleep, etc. Once your body is attuned to this practice, the mind will automatically start working on breathing during stressful situations without any effort.

Anxiety, the illness of our time, comes primarily from our inability to live in the present moment-Thich Nhat Hanh

CHAPTER 18

CREATING MIRACLES IN LIFE

You are connected to the same creative energy that designed the universe. The power that formed galaxies, stars, and planets is present within you as well. If such energy can shape the vast cosmos, it can certainly support you in creating the everyday things you desire—whether it's financial growth, opportunities, or a life of abundance.

When you begin to see clearly how your mind and heart operate, you gain the wisdom to transform the storms of destructive emotions. Compassion softens the heart, instills courage, and gently dissolves fear. From that place of inner stillness, intelligence becomes sharper and more luminous. True strength lies in remaining calm—not lifeless or indifferent, but calm in a way that vibrates with awareness and vitality.

It is of utmost importance to understand the working of the mind. Mind is the foremost factor responsible for our success or failure, happiness or miseries. Before we continue with this chapter, it is recommended to ensure that the concepts elaborated in previous chapters are properly understood. If in any kind of doubt, re-read the previous chapters.

The concepts explained in those chapters form the basis of what we are going to learn now. Hence, if you want to get wealth, health, success, or any other thing in life and that too within a limited amount of time, then please take extra effort to read again to gain clarity.

If you want your life energy to attune with the universal energy for getting positive results, then the concept of gratitude, compassion, and charity, as explained earlier, is to be understood and put into daily practical use. Add to this at least 10 to 15 minutes of meditation sessions twice a day, and you will experience the change. As can be seen from previous chapters, it is not difficult to incorporate these things into our daily lives. Only a little effort, and soon it will become a habit and automatically become your daily routine.

Ready! Ok, let's continue.

Conditioning and Reconditioning of Mind

I remember my initial stage of practicing mindfulness meditation. I used to follow, whenever possible, the routine of observing the bodily movements consciously.

One day while taking a shower, I realised that singing happened automatically while in the bathroom. Whenever inside the bathroom, the songs unknowingly came to my lips. Even when I was in a bad mood, and there was no chance of singing, the singing happened. How could this happen? How can the singing happen without my permission? Well, this has not occurred in a single day. It happened years ago when I first sang in the bathroom, and the repetitions thereafter made it into a habit. This daily habit has gradually taken hold of my mind over the years (to sing while taking a shower) and forces the body to react. Most of our habits happen over time due to regular repetition. It can thus be understood that the mind gets magnetized by the thoughts or actions repeatedly fed into it.

Just as singing in the shower is a result of a habit.

Similarly, being rich is due to our habits!

Being happy is also because of our habits!

As explained in previous chapters, our mind is preoccupied with negative emotions and fear; further, we keep on adding to it through our habitual negative thought patterns. These repetitions of emotions and thoughts are responsible for our failures or miseries. Fear and retaining negativity is the basic nature of our mind, and hence, efforts are required to break this conditioning pattern.

What you say doesn't just communicate—it conditions your mind. By repeatedly feeding it with constructive and encouraging thoughts, you gradually reprogram its patterns. However, we need to be very careful about the words that we use for reconditioning our minds. Sometimes the words that we use appear to be positive, but they are not.

Let's do an exercise. Read the following sentences loudly 3 times;

I will not fail

I will succeed.

Which sentence generates positivity? The meaning of both these sentences is the same, but their effect on our way of thinking varies. Well, 'I will succeed' generates positivity.

Whenever a child is told not to be afraid of the dark, he ends up being more terrified.

Let's take an example of a person who is learning to swim. As we all know, it is natural for the learner to drown in water at the initial stage of learning. If the learner, while swimming, feels that he is drowning and tries to pacify his mind by saying, "I will not drown," then the chances of his drowning increase. Mind senses the desperation behind his thought of 'not drowning' and sends out a fear signal. The mind realizes that something is wrong and tries to help by trying to work out all possible ways to protect that person. But the mind is unable to judge the very short time frame available to work out those solutions. The desperation adds to the negativity of this fear, and their combination gives a more negative result. The person will therefore get drawn into the water. Though the words "I will not drown" appear to be positive, they are not.

What did we learn?

From the above paragraphs, we learned that the mind gets magnetized by the thoughts repeatedly fed into it. This tendency of the mind can be used to recondition it by repeatedly feeding positive input into it. This is called autosuggestion.

Secondly, we learned that since the mind's basic nature is to be fearful, we should avoid negative prefixes or words like not, don't, etc, for giving autosuggestion for reconditioning the mind.

Therefore, instead of saying 'I will not fail,' use the wording

'I will succeed.'

Instead of saying 'I'm not afraid,' use the wording 'I'm fearless.

Negatives are to be strictly avoided. Only positive affirmations are to be used for autosuggestion.

Though the sentence may appear positive, the use of negative negative-sounding verb, i.e, 'not', confuses the negative judgmental ability of the mind and thereby creates a more negative result.

Make it a point to remember these properties of the mind, and we can use them to create miracles in life.

Re-read and Not to Miss Summary

To align your personal energy with the rhythm of the universe, nurture daily practices such as gratitude, compassion, generosity, and meditation.

- The mind becomes what it repeatedly thinks and does—your habits silently sculpt your results.
- Negative conditioning, such as fear, doubt, or constant negativity, drags life toward frustration and suffering. Positive conditioning, on the other hand, opens the door to growth, fulfillment, and joy.
- Autosuggestion works as a tool to reshape the mind. By consistently repeating empowering thoughts, you slowly train your inner dialogue to support you instead of limiting you.

- Always choose affirmations that declare success directly (e.g., "I will succeed") rather than in a negative form (e.g., "I will not fail").
- Avoid negations such as "not," "don't," or "never," because the mind absorbs the emotional charge of the words and often reinforces the very fear you wish to escape.
- When the mind is guided with clarity, persistence, and positivity, it begins to deliver the results you seek.
- Even small, steady efforts lead to transformation—over time, positive conditioning becomes second nature.
- Words carry power. Speak to your mind with conviction, clarity, and encouragement, and it will respond in kind.

CHAPTER 19

WEALTH CREATION & FREEDOM PLAN

A small portion of life needs to be sincerely dedicated to our prime goal, and the results thus obtained will work for the rest of life.

The mind itself does not think independently—it is shaped by what we feed it with genuine emotion and belief. Every outcome in your life today is the reflection of the beliefs you have carried within. Limiting beliefs quietly build a destiny of struggle, while empowering beliefs pave the way for freedom and success.

In essence, to change your life, you must first change the way you think.

The continuous stream of thoughts, channelized towards that one goal, gives the desired outcome. Magnetize your mind with that thought. Let it become a passion.

Think big: We set limits on our thinking and restrict our growth.

Our approach toward wealth creation is very cautious. We fear to think big as far as wealth creation is concerned. Thinking is free, so why do we restrict our thoughts to mediocrity? Why can't I think about owning a high-end car instead of aiming for the low-segment one? Why can't I imagine residing in a spacious house in my preferred location instead of struggling to move out of that rented property? Thinking big is the first important step in this journey of abundance and prosperity. Educational qualification does not matter in your journey to success.

Motivate through imagination: ***Low aim and excuses are the greatest hurdles in our progress.***

Imagination is the most powerful tool. It can also be used for self-motivation. Motivate yourself daily by imagining the joy that you and your family will experience after you earn the desired riches.

Think about the problems that will be resolved and imagine the feeling of being free of that problem. Think about your family goals that can now be achieved.

Imagine looking into the eyes of your mother and feeling the pride therein about your success. Imagine the happiness that your father will exhibit after seeing your progress.

Imagine the reaction of relatives or friends who till now took you for granted.

Imagine the reaction of the people who underestimated you and how you proved them wrong.

Imagine the things that you could now buy and satisfy your family's needs.

Imagine the exotic locations where you could travel to now. Feel the bliss.

The list is endless. Choose the one that suits you best or create a new one as per your requirement.

Please, please start thinking about the joy of achievement.

Don't just imagine. Feel it. Stay motivated.

If you are still unsure about the effect of thoughts on your life, then take a pause and look back on your thought patterns in this life so far. It will be amply clear that whatever you are today is because of the way you think.

Don't strive for perfection, make a start. Waiting for things to be perfect and aiming to create perfect things takes away our precious time.

I would like to repeat a small portion of the writing from the preface of this book. The repetition is to highlight the importance of taking the first step.

We say that life is a struggle. But most of the time, the struggle is because of a lack of effort. Ask yourself a question about the efforts taken so far to improve your present situation. In most cases, we do nothing and then call it a struggle. The important thing is to start. Just move and initiate action.

Suppose you have moved into a new house and there is lots of cleaning to be done and clutter to be arranged; what would you do?

Would you just sit back and look at the mess because clearing and arranging it is a time-consuming and tedious job?

You will work on it because there is no other option, as you have to stay in that house. In that case, you will start from somewhere and move from one item to another. Slowly and gradually, the clutter gets arranged as the brain automatically guides you in the process. Eventually, the work is done and everything falls into place.

The same is true about our lives. The problems and obstacles are due to the mental clutter that we accumulate.

Break the lucky unlucky Jinx

The fault, dear Brutus, is not in our stars, but ourselves

– William Shakespeare

I have seen many people who carry this mental superstition of being unlucky or doomed. This greatly affects their success prospects. As explained in the previous chapters, whatever we sincerely believe manifests in our lives. If a person thinks he is unlucky, then he is creating situations for his misfortune. Also, the person takes it for granted that being unlucky is the reason for his problems. The effort to succeed ends there because he thinks about being helpless before the luck factor.

Also, don't call yourself lucky, because in your mind, this creates an impression that you may be unlucky at some other time.

Use the techniques provided in this book to recondition your mind. Never say I'm unlucky or I'm lucky. Both these sentences have negative implications in the long run. This is because our mind associates lucky and unlucky with a mysterious force beyond our control and thinks that, since things are beyond our control, we can do nothing about it. Luck or unlucky is immeasurable and is not concrete.

Believe in your efforts and change the situation. Also, remember that efforts should be directed towards measurable goals to be achieved within a certain time frame. Example: Earning 5 Lakh rupees in 90 days. Here, the amount you want to earn and the time frame in which you want those earnings are defined.

Going back to the Lucky-unlucky conflict, never use these words for yourself or anybody else. Instead of saying I'm lucky, say I'm blessed. Not only during good times but also in normal or trying situations, continue to count yourself as blessed and keep repeating to yourself. Make it a habit to say I'm blessed often, and soon things will begin to change for good.

Where to earn the money from? How to find the right opportunity to earn money?

The New Wealth Landscape

The world today is brimming with opportunities. Wealth is no longer created only by traditional businesses, offices, or shops. The digital economy has opened doors that our grandparents couldn't even imagine. This book was written during the COVID pandemic, when the whole world was experiencing a severe setback. However, as per the 10th Edition of the Hurun Global Rich List 2021, the world added 607 new billionaires or more than three billionaires in two days. The year 2020 has seen the biggest wealth increase of that decade despite the COVID pandemic (As reported in the Hindu newspaper.)

You need to find out the way through which you can take your share of riches.

If you have a skill, then polish it and make it presentable. Convince people about how you can solve their problems through your service or product. Be genuine in your efforts and provide quality service.

Look around and you will find people making money through various means. Make use of digital platforms, social media and artificial intelligence(AI) for availing opportunities that never existed before.

Money is always in circulation in the market. Find a way to grab your share of wealth.

The conventional way of earning money by doing jobs or setting up offices and shops is also slowly being replaced in this digital age. In today's digital world, one can earn money around the clock and that too with little or no investment. You can create digital online systems and opportunities that allow wealth to flow to you even while you rest.

Whether it is a conventional type of business or a digital one, great opportunities are available. It is much easier to earn money today than ever before due to digital outreach.

Closing Reflection

Don't remain a spectator to other people's achievements or sit around hoping for a chance to favor you. Begin exactly where you are, make the most of the resources already in your hands, and dare to envision dreams larger than you ever thought possible.

CHAPTER 20

THE TWO-STEP METHOD – POUR OUT & FILL IN

"Continuous effort—not strength or intelligence—is the key to unlocking our potential."

– Winston Churchill

The Principle of Pouring Out

One of the great secrets of success is this: before you can fill your cup with fresh water, you must first pour out the stale water already inside. In life, too, if we want abundance, creativity, and success to enter, we must release the things that block our growth.

This is where the Two-Step Method begins:

1. Pour out what no longer serves you.
2. Fill in what will empower and uplift you.

Thinking Differently: The Path Less Taken

Your chances of success multiply when you choose a completely new path—or when you walk a familiar path in a new way. The advantage of doing things differently is simple: there is little or no competition there.

If you stumble upon a unique idea that genuinely solves people's problems, you become a trendsetter. And even if you cannot discover something new, you can reimagine the old with your personal twist.

History remembers those who innovate..

The Power of Inspiration

I personally get fired up when I hear the stories of people who broke the mold. Their journeys awaken my imagination and give me courage. That's why I recommend regularly listening to successful people who followed unusual routes. TED talks, YouTube interviews, and podcasts are full of such gems.

But here's the key: don't just consume information. Pay attention to what resonates with you and apply it in your own life. We live in an age of information overload; wisdom lies in filtering the noise and focusing on what expands your possibilities.

A Story of Pouring Out Fear of Ridicule & Filling In Passion

In 1984, a young man shocked everyone around him by choosing to become a cook. At that time in India, cooking was stereotyped as "women's work." Friends mocked him, calling him bawarchi. However, he was determined to fulfil his passion. While doing hotel management, he realised that the teachers were hesitant to give out their secret tricks about cooking and imparted only conventional knowledge. Those teachers were afraid that disclosing their secret tips would make their students more successful as compared to themselves. He then promised himself that whenever he became a successful cook, he would give away all his knowledge to the seekers. He worked hard to gain that knowledge and got a job in one of the hotels. One day, while standing in the hotel lobby to give instructions to his subordinates, one of his seniors asked him to go back to the kitchen and not hang around in the lobby; he was further told that the place of a chef is in the kitchen. He then realised the sorry state of Indian women, who were confined to a kitchen job and were reminded that their place was in the kitchen. The next promise he made to himself was to break this notion of women being primarily associated with the kitchen and bring honour to their culinary skills.

He kept his promise and started to share his cooking knowledge and secret tips by starting a cookery show 'Khana Khazana', which became the longest-running show of its kind in Asia; the program reached audiences in 120 nations, and by 2010 it had attracted over half a billion viewers worldwide.

He brought glamour to the cooking profession and became a celebrity chef, entrepreneur, and famous television personality. He is none other than Sanjeev Kapoor, recipient of many national and international awards, which include 'Padma Shri', the fourth-highest civilian award in India. He changed people's perspectives on cooking and inspired a whole lot of people to take up cooking as a profession. Let me quote what he said in one of his video talks;

No matter what we do, no matter what we choose to do, if we focus more on what we are giving rather than what we are getting, then our success is assured. The joy of giving is far superior to the joy of receiving. This is my success formula. What I get just follows. I have never thought about or worried about what I'm getting. So, think in terms of what you can give rather than what you receive - Sanjeev Kapoor

Untapped Potential: A Story of Wasted Genius

In my own first job as an electrical engineer, I worked with a middle-aged assistant who had no formal education but astonishing skill with electrical circuits. His problem-solving ability was extraordinary. Yet, he restricted his genius to routine company tasks.

He could have created inventions, patents, or even a business of his own. But he didn't. Perhaps fear, laziness, or a craving for security held him back. His brilliance remained buried under the ordinary.

That incident taught me a painful truth: **potential unused is potential wasted.**

Why People Settle for Mediocrity?

I often wondered: Why do people fail to use their gifts of talent? The answer lies in the mindset of following the same trend as the society or the majority of people follow. We conform and try to follow the same old path. In India, we are trained to chase secure jobs rather than take risks. Families encourage "safety" over "exploration." As a result, many brilliant minds live and die in mediocrity.

The universe doesn't work on accidents. If I'm born as a human, then it's not an accident, and if nature has chosen me for this form, it has empowered me with the resources to face life challenges. In short, nobody is born without potential. The only question is about understanding and utilizing it.

Our family and the company we keep also play a huge part in defining our mentality. The example of the person above underlines our tendency to play it safe. We refuse to accept challenges, and until we do not dare to think big, we may continue to live a mediocre life.

A very important point to be noted- Trending on a different path does not mean that you go out and invent the wheel. The majority of us are unaware of our abilities or lack the will to put those abilities to use. If you are aware of your skills, then use those skills for greater success by adding a new and exciting element to them.

Some people fail to see their own potential, while others fail to put it to good use. Accordingly, I found that people can be broadly divided into the following five categories;

Go through the following details and try to identify the category (type of person) you are.

Five Types of People;

1. The Natural Achievers – Born with an inner drive and unwavering focus. Success feels natural. (Einstein, Helen Keller, Sachin Tendulkar.) Rare, but inspiring.
2. The Day-to-Day Survivors – Focused only on immediate needs. A daily wage worker or one who depends on a monthly salary. Most people fall here, leading ordinary lives.

3. The Crisis Learners – They discover their strength only after an emergency shakes them up. The crisis awakens them to realize their potential and serves as a stepping stone to build lifelong resources for a successful life.
4. The Crisis Forgetters – Same as above, but once the crisis passes, they slip back to old ways, wasting lessons learned.
5. The Excuse-Makers – No motivation, always blaming luck or circumstances. They spend their lives in complaint, not creation.

Which one are you?

The Things You Must Pour Out

To reach new heights, you must begin with an open and receptive mind.. The four biggest blocks are:

1. **Excuses** – Excuses may shield your pride for a moment, but they silently sabotage your tomorrow.
2. **Inaction** – Doing nothing is the fastest way to fail.
3. **Postponement** – Tomorrow becomes never.
4. **Fear** – Fear of failure, of rejection, of the unknown.

Pour these out, consciously. Write them down, acknowledge them, and then let them go.

The Filling In- When you clear away the clutter, you make room for new possibilities to unfold. As soon as the desire to succeed magnetizes your mind, your hidden abilities begin to emerge.

The next step is learning what to fill in—new habits, empowering thoughts, and courageous action. That's the subject of the next chapter.

Empowerment Insight

Don't underestimate yourself. The cup of your life is waiting to be refilled. But first, pour out what no longer serves you.

CHAPTER 21

THINGS TO FILL IN

If you are afraid to leave your comfort zone, then be prepared to live a life of discomfort forever.

This chapter is dedicated to Napoleon Hill, the legendary author of Think and Grow Rich, whose timeless work has inspired countless authors, leaders, and trainers—including myself. His insights on autosuggestion opened my eyes to the power of the subconscious mind and played a defining role in whatever little success I have achieved in my life.

Hill's wisdom is simple yet profound: we become what we repeatedly feed to our minds. Success, freedom, and abundance are not accidents; they are outcomes of deliberate mental programming.

Why Fill In?

In the previous chapter, we learned about the things we must pour out—excuses, inaction, postponement, and fear. But once the vessel is emptied, it must be filled with something purposeful, powerful, and positive. That is where autosuggestions—deliberate, repeated affirmations—come into play.

The truth is, your mind doesn't have a mind of its own. It accepts whatever is fed to it consistently and with emotion. If you keep feeding it doubts, fears, and excuses, it will faithfully manifest mediocrity. But if you repeatedly plant seeds of faith, vision, and success, your subconscious will begin to act in alignment with those seeds.

This is the essence of the "Fill In" method.

Step One: Write It Down

Don't just dream in your head—write it down. No matter how absurd, big, or distant it may seem today, put it on paper. A written goal is like a contract with your future self. It transforms a wish into a commitment.

Speak your goal aloud at least three times a day. Repeat it in the morning, in the evening, and whenever doubts creep in. Initially, your mind may resist. You may feel silly. But persistence is key. Over time, the repetition rewires your subconscious until belief replaces doubt.

A Real-Life Example

During one of my training sessions, I met a Human Resources (HR) professional in his early fifties. After decades of chasing responsibilities, he realized he was neither fabulously wealthy nor truly satisfied. Though he held a high-ranking position in a reputed organization, stress and workload were draining him. He longed for freedom but feared financial insecurity.

When we calculated his financial path, we found that if he continued in his job until retirement, he would earn roughly ₹2 Crores (₹20 million) over the next 7 years, despite working up to 10 to 12 hours a day, five days each week.

Then I asked him a simple question:

"What if you could earn the same amount in just 2 years by doing something you love?"

That changed everything.

He realized he could use his natural gift as a communicator and trainer to create digital courses, coach people, and eventually step out of the job. With this plan, he wasn't just earning money—he was buying his freedom.

His Fill-In Formula

I guided him to structure his autosuggestions using five steps:

1. State the Goal – What do you want?
2. Fix the Timeline – By when do you want it?

3. Define the Value Exchange – What service or product will you give in return?
4. Visualize and Feel – See yourself already living the success.
5. Commit to Giving Back – Decide how you will share your blessings with others.

Here's how his daily autosuggestion looked:

"I am earning ₹2 Crores in the next 24 months by providing life-changing mind training techniques to my clients. They use my guidance to create abundance, prosperity, and freedom in their lives. I use this wealth to resign from my present job at the age of 53 and live a life of choice and freedom.

I experience and deeply feel the flow of wealth, the abundance it creates, and the happiness it brings to me and my loved ones. I am blessed, and I wholeheartedly spend 20% of my income to help others overcome their struggles and miseries. May all beings be blessed! May I be blessed as well!"

He was asked to:

- Write this statement twice a day (morning and evening).
- Speak it out loud with genuine feeling.

- Carry a pocket card with the statement and revisit it thrice daily.
- Visualize the journey: training audiences, receiving appreciation, enjoying abundance, driving his dream car, relaxing in his dream home, and celebrating freedom with loved ones.

Your Turn: Craft Your Freedom Plan

Whether you are in a private job, government service, running a business, or even struggling to find direction, this method applies to you.

Start by asking:

- What exact amount of money do I desire, and by what time frame?
- What skill, service, or product will I exchange?
- What does my freedom life look and feel like?
- How will I give back?

Even if implementation feels far away, at least have your plan ready. Writing it down is the first act of courage.

The Enemy Within: Excuses

When you begin this exercise, your mind will likely push back. It may whisper:

- "I don't have the right abilities."
- "I'm too old to begin something new."

- "Earning two crores in two years? That's unrealistic."
- "My English isn't good enough."
- "I don't have the funds or resources."

But remember—these are not truths, they're just excuses. Excuses are the bricks that build the walls of an average life. Tear those walls down. Let your hunger for freedom burn brighter than the excuses that try to hold you back.

Determination vs. Desperation

One important caution: be determined, not desperate. Determination empowers, but desperation drains. When desperate, you try to control everything and end up controlled by frustration.

Here's a simple test: After 2 weeks of practicing autosuggestions, ask yourself—do I feel more motivated and optimistic, or stressed and anxious?

- If stressed, you are rushing, forcing, or doubting. Stop, breathe, and reset.
- If uplifted and positive, you are on the right path.

Autosuggestions should make your heart lighter, not heavier.

Action Step

Freedom will never be found through waiting, wishing, or complaining. It will come from writing, repeating, visualizing, and acting with faith.

Pour out your fears. Fill in your faith. And remember—a calm mind, a proper plan, and determined effort are the keys to creating the life you dream of.

CHAPTER 22

OVERCOMING HURDLES ON THE PATH TO SUCCESS

The seed of growth lies in challenges

Once you have decided on your goal, find out the one big factor that is stopping you from progressing or from achieving your goal. The factor in most cases is either fear of failure or procrastination, or both.

In my case, the biggest factor was procrastination. Though I knew my goal and the path towards achieving that goal, I kept on postponing the journey. The reason for this was a secure job with adequate cash flow to maintain a suitable standard of living. But the realization that I could earn greater riches and could live a much more fulfilling life made me wake up from my slumber of inaction and get rid of the habit of procrastination. I chose to organize my life and focus on what truly excites me.

What is procrastination?

Procrastination means deliberately delaying tasks that should be completed.

Why do we procrastinate or postpone things to tomorrow?

This can be roughly understood through Parkinson's Law.

According to Parkinson's First Law, work naturally stretches to occupy all the time allotted for it.

This simply means that we try to stretch and fill in the work or goal into the available period. We keep on postponing the work till the end of the scheduled time. This is the reason we start preparing for the exams only when the exam dates approach. This is true for most of our activities. In offices, it has been observed that employees tend to arrive late and leave early if no proper monitoring system is in place. After the installation of biometric or digital thumb impression systems in the offices, the same employees started to arrive and leave on time. Their timely arrival was now monitored by the system, and suddenly they became disciplined and started respecting the time.

When in school, we had a definite timetable, we reached our school on time and attended the classes, and completed the projects as per schedule, this way we made ourselves ready for the examinations. We humans, therefore, developed this tendency to do things only when pushed and monitored by someone.

In the later part of life, after completing our education, we are left on our own; there is nobody to push or motivate. Unlike school, there is no timetable now as there are no exams to face as such. Hence, we procrastinate. We forget that the examination of life is much tougher than the one we faced in our schools.

In early youth, we are full of energy and overflowing with energy. We dream about achievements in the future. Since there is no one to set a goal or plan for us, we procrastinate. As time passes and we fail to achieve the desired success, we start the blame games.

We start blaming each and everyone around us, except ourselves. We blame the people, the circumstances, and the bad luck that has befallen.

Due to responsibilities, we may take up jobs that come our way just to sustain the responsibilities of family life. The job is just for survival, and we end up spending a major portion of our lives doing it. Stepping out of our comfort zone feels intimidating.

We forget to live life. We just survive.

This is because we do not set a goal, we do not plan. Also, just a goal and a plan are not sufficient; it must be backed up by a non-procrastinating desire to succeed.

Just like the school days, set up a written timetable for yourself, set up a goal, determine the time frame within which you intend to achieve that goal, and do not procrastinate.

Some people set a goal and know the way to implement it. But then they procrastinate. This hesitation often comes either from the fear of failing or from simple inertia. Procrastination is one major reason for people not achieving their goals.

How to overcome procrastination?

Respecting time is the solution.

As discussed above, no external system should be required for you to do things on time. Filling the available time with inactivity and then suddenly starting preparation at the last moment should be avoided. This is a matter of practice and needs special efforts. Greater things cannot be achieved without dedicated efforts. There is no single method or solution to overcome the habit of procrastination. However, one can follow the following methods, which I found beneficial;

1. Getting up early in the morning.
2. Journaling.

Getting up early

We are all aware of the advantages of rising early. As Benjamin Franklin wisely said, "Go to bed early and rise early, and you will enjoy health, wealth, and wisdom." However, getting up earlier than the habitual time is not a simple task. As per my personal experience, it is possible to control almost all things, including hunger, for some time, but when the urge to sleep strikes, it is next to impossible to keep it at bay. You may have also experienced this while studying, attending a meeting or a seminar where the speech is making you fall asleep and you are trying to keep awake.

According to the Wall Street Journal, 4 am is the most productive hour to wake up. But, if your regular wake-up time is 7 am and I ask you to get up at 4 am, then there are chances that you may discard this book or give up reading it. Some of us may succeed in getting up early on a few occasions, but to sustain it and make it a lifelong habit is difficult. Hence. I would suggest a practical and viable method to wake up early.

Initially, try to wake up at least one hour before your regular wake-up time, and once this habit is developed, gradually try to rise earlier. Utilize this extra time for meditating (sit down and observe the movement of air through your nostrils, the air is coming in, the air is going out - just observe the natural flow without trying to control it) for 15 minutes, writing down your goals, repeating the affirmations about the things you want to achieve and the person you want to be. Go out for a walk for at least 10-15 minutes. It is during this walk that those fresh ideas will start appearing in your mind. Do this regularly without giving it a miss.

This is the method that I found useful for myself, and I hope it will be beneficial to others too. Once you experience the benefit, it will motivate you to get up earlier. This will also reduce your tendency to hasten, as this extra time will allow you the space to accommodate your schedule. Gradually, after getting habituated to this routine, the next step would be to try and rise earlier than the present wake-up time.

It is said that 'early risers are achievers' and various studies have proved it to be true. Most of the highly successful people in the history of mankind were/are early risers. Hence, make your dream bigger than excuses. Let the passion for your dream outweigh the temptation to stay in bed.

Journaling

This will help you in understanding the factors that are unnecessarily taking up your time and the areas in which you need to work and spend more time. Take note of even the innocent-looking habit that takes up your considerable time.

Take an ordinary notebook or a diary. Do not worry about grammar or handwriting, because concentrating on it would further take up some time. Just ensure that your writing is readable, as it will be required for future reference.

Note down the following points in your journal;

1) **Activities that are unnecessarily taking up your time.**
   In my case, I had this habit of reading multiple newspapers and watching TV news to keep myself updated with current affairs. This habit continued since my college days, when I was preparing for various competitive exams and needed to keep myself updated. But now, after more than a couple of decades in service, there was no need for me to continue with this activity. So, I discontinued the subscription to multiple newspapers and also stopped watching the news (unless something very important is happening). This is apart from the fact that the

news channels are no more worth watching. Also, now I just glance at the newspaper headlines and read only the relevant ones. The time that I now spend on social media is also restricted. You may also identify the activities that are not worth your time and reduce the time spent on them.

2) **Create a to-do list to set your priorities clearly,** Write down the tasks that truly deserve your attention. Divide these priorities into two parts, minor and major. Work immediately on the minor priorities and strike them out of the to-do list, then concentrate on the major ones. Face them; find out a way to conclude them. This will help you in finishing your priorities in a time-bound manner, thereby breaking the habit of procrastination. If, despite all possible efforts, you are unable to finish a task due to some unavoidable reasons then don't get discouraged. Some tasks may remain unfinished, and it is fine.

Also, take note of behavioural issues that interfere with your day-to-day performance. This may include distraction, procrastination, anger, smoking etc.

Rate yourself on a scale of 0 to 5 as per the response or reaction you exhibited towards that event on that day. No need to feel guilty if you score badly, just go on rating yourself genuinely on a day-to-day basis, and there is a high chance of you being surprised by the improved score after a few days.

Why does this improvement happen? The reason is, your mind now takes daily note of your issue and unconsciously feels bad about it, tries to find out a solution. So far, there was no data on your daily reactions, but now you are keeping a record and realizing the areas in which you need to work.

So now that you have a goal, a non-procrastinating attitude, and a plan to achieve that goal, what else is needed?

Patience! Patience is the one thing that we need to maintain throughout this journey of moving toward success.

Focus on your goal and maintain patience!

Work on the things if you want the things to work for you.

Key Takeaway

Don't wait for external pressure to push you. Build your own timetable, respect your time, rise early, journal your journey, and most importantly—stay patient. Success is the reward of disciplined persistence.

CHAPTER 23

BALANCING LIFE

Don't hold the bird too tightly, or it might die

The above quote does not apply only to love and relationships but also to the materialistic things that we continue to cling to. As Lao Tzu said, *"The treasure of life is missed by those who continue to hold on."*

Your achievements should contribute to your freedom. If this is not happening, then your achievements are indirectly hampering your freedom and joy of living.

I remember one incident from around 2 years back. A youngster from a wealthy family came for counselling. He was unable to find the purpose of his life and was feeling depressed. Since earning money was not a necessity, the only thing that he did was splurge on the riches of his parents. Ample money was available for him to spend. The problem is that we are being told to 'enjoy life 'instead of 'live life'. Enjoying life is a mirage because we cannot enjoy anything for a longer duration, and enjoying our whole life is impossible. Our life is balanced by dualities, and therefore, sooner or later, our mind will again find reasons to complain and feel dissatisfied. Even the joy experienced through our so-called greatest achievements is temporary. The youngster, as mentioned above, tried to enjoy life through money, but he soon realised its limitations and therefore struggled to find purpose in life. The desire to enjoy life sows the seeds of future miseries.

As told earlier, we tend to look at the larger picture of life, thereby missing the smaller and minute aspects of our existence. When we desire happiness, we are indirectly considering ourselves unhappy and continue to wait for that happiness in some distant future. The distant future never arrives. The gloom of dissatisfaction and sorrow unknowingly form layers over our minds, thereby causing never-ending unhappiness.

So, should we not think about enjoyment or happiness?

Let's think about this in another way. Good things are regularly happening to us daily, but we do not pay attention to those moments of good happenings, and our mind misses recording them. On the contrary, we immediately react to even a minor undesired event and keep on adding to our unhappiness quantum.

Thích Nhất Hạnh reminds us with a simple example: when you are suffering from a toothache, you rush to the dentist for urgent relief. In that painful moment, you clearly recognize that the absence of a toothache is true happiness. Yet once the pain is gone, we rarely value the state of "no toothache" and quickly take it for granted.

Thích Nhất Hạnh uses the example to show how often we overlook everyday happiness. When pain strikes, we desperately seek relief. In that moment, we realize that the simple state of not having pain is a blessing. But once the pain disappears, we quickly forget and no longer appreciate it. This is how life often works—we take peace, comfort, and good health for granted until they are missing.

Once we train our minds to appreciate the nice little things in our lives, life begins to change. We wait for something magnificent to happen, thereby missing the small sunshine moments in our lives. Everything is a result of our habits. Habit formation takes place due to our reaction to whatever happens around us. As explained in the previous chapters, there are various reasons to feel happy; recollect those moments regularly, such that the quantum of happy moments recorded by our mind increases, and soon more events of a positive nature will begin to take place. This requires practice and effort initially, but once your mind becomes habitual, it will effortlessly work for you as per the most prominent pattern (happiness or unhappiness) it has been conditioned to.

Once you learn the way to stay happy, you will start getting glimpses of a higher state of mind, which is beyond happiness.

The Story of an Unhappy Man

There is one incident in Buddha's life. A person visited Buddha and asked,

"Would I become happy after becoming your disciple?"

Buddha smiled and replied, "Firstly, you cannot become a disciple with terms and conditions. A disciple needs to surrender without any desire; even a desire for happiness is not expected."

"Secondly, about your question, whether you would be happy after becoming my disciple! Let me clarify that if you sincerely follow my path, you would be neither happy nor unhappy."

Here, the Buddha is talking about the state of mind that is beyond happiness or unhappiness. This is the state of bliss. Bliss cannot be explained in words; it can only be experienced. Our aim should be to raise the consciousness to the level of experiencing bliss.

Balancing success with satisfaction will lead to a wholesome life.

Life Summary

Life is a continuous search for balance, between clinging and releasing, between striving for success and enjoying contentment, between seeking happiness and embracing acceptance. When we cling too tightly to achievements, possessions, or relationships, they stop bringing us joy and instead become burdens. True freedom comes when our achievements support life's flow rather than restrict it.

By cultivating habits of appreciation, we gradually train the mind to focus on happiness rather than misery.

CHAPTER 24

HOW TO DEAL WITH FUTURE CHALLENGES?

(TIPS TO DEAL WITH THE FAST-CHANGING WORLD)

Let the world change, but the laws of nature will always remain the same. Follow those laws and you will be taken care of.

The day-to-day challenges in today's digital world are different from what they used to be in the past. Today, our life revolves around electronic technology and our mind is continuously exposed to digital data from computers, mobile phones, televisions, and satellite channels. This affects the way we think, and as discussed in earlier chapters, our life is the product of our thinking. Hence, it is very essential to guard our minds against this illusory digital world. The physical world itself is an illusion, and now we are creating more layers of illusion in it by using technology. The gap between the real and the illusion is fast disappearing.

The age of traditional education is getting replaced with new advancements, and the changes henceforth would be quick and frequent. The industrial revolution is being taken over by the digital and service sectors. The 9 -5 job will be replaced by working from a distant place at any required time. The ball is already set in motion, and nobody can stay away from it. While matching the fast-paced world with new emerging technologies, the world would be subjected to new physical and mental health-related challenges.

The good thing is that digital technology provides greater earning resources to people of all intellectual levels. Creating digital tools that make money around the clock without your intervention is now possible. Creating wealth would be easy, but coping with the everyday routine and challenges would be difficult.

How to deal with this fast-changing world?

One of the most serious drawbacks of modern living is that it has harmed silence, which is necessary for inner peace. Our tranquillity has been jeopardised. A state of inner stillness is essential, not only for the healthy functioning of body and mind but also for the process of deep healing. Our multitasking and hurried habits disrupt our inner equilibrium, resulting in bodily and emotional problems.

There are situations in life when we want the chaos around us to stop, the chaos of thoughts, the chaos of happenings, but we do not know how to stop them. We desire to be left alone. We isolate ourselves from the world. Physically, we isolate ourselves from the world, but what about the mind? The chattering of the mind and the chaos inside the head still go on, and just physical isolation will not help; instead, the continuous disturbance of the mind may further cause problems.

Modern technology might be helping us in our day-to-day work, but it is also taking a heavy toll on the way we think and behave. We are facing problems related to;

1. Short attention span.
2. Tendency to react fast, causing emotional outbursts.
3. Memory retention issues.
4. Sleep disorders.

Research claimed that our average attention span has shrunk to around 8 seconds, down from 12 seconds at the start of the century. To make the finding even more striking, it was compared with a goldfish, which is said to hold focus for about 9 seconds. Whether or not this comparison is scientifically flawless, the message is powerful: human beings are losing the ability to stay present.

Think about it. We scroll endlessly on our phones, jumping from one post to another, rarely finishing an article, video, or even a thought before moving on. In many ways, our restless minds have become like a channel remote, constantly flipping without settling. The numbers may be debated, but the reality is clear—our attention is weaker than it used to be, and reclaiming it has become one of the great challenges of modern life.

The Internet has played a huge role in affecting the way we think and live. We have become habitual about keeping ourselves preoccupied with meaningless activities. We become restless when idle and then habitually switch from social media to OTT platforms. This is taking a huge toll on our ability to relax and access the silence from within.

Peace is not possible without silence from within. We have unknowingly compromised our peace. We are trapped between the real and unreal. Digital technology is further reducing the gap between virtual space and real life. The day is not far away when we may be unable to distinguish between what is real, and virtual and that may create irresolvable psychological issues.

Since we have no option but to adapt to these changes, we need to learn to associate and dissociate ourselves from the technology as and when required. Here, we need to learn to calm down from within to access our inner selves. Here comes the role of silence.

Many people assume that those who design our digital devices and platforms encourage their own families to use them freely. Surprisingly, the opposite is often true. For example, Steve Jobs once shared in a New York Times interview that his children were not allowed to use iPads at home. Bill Gates also revealed that he postponed giving his kids smartphones until their teenage years and enforced strict screen-time rules. Similar sentiments have been echoed by several Silicon Valley executives, who intentionally limit digital exposure within their households. The very people who pioneered these innovations understand how addictive technology can become and take active measures to protect their families from its overuse. This contrast highlights an important truth: while digital tools can be powerful and useful, they must be handled with awareness and boundaries.

Pause & Reflect – Your Digital Boundaries.

Both your time and your mental energy are valuable resources. Use it wisely.

Self-Check: How many hours a day do you spend on screens purely for leisure?

Choose One Rule: If you were to set just one healthy boundary (for example: no phones at the dinner table or no screens an hour before sleep), which would have the biggest positive impact on your life?

Action Step: Write this boundary down and commit to practicing it for one week. Pay attention to the way your thoughts, emotions, and energy levels change.

Remember: Even the creators of today's most powerful digital tools set limits. You can too.

CHAPTER 25

THE POWER OF SILENCE

We suffer in silence. Let's now learn to heal in silence.

True peace begins when the inner noise is quietened, for silence is the bridge between chaos and calm, between pain and peace. Healing, is not always about doing; sometimes it is about sitting quietly and allowing life to mend you.

In embracing silence, we give our inner self permission to heal itself and discover that stillness is the deepest source of strength.

Understanding the Role of Silence in Daily Life

Not only for dealing with the challenges associated with digital technology, but also for day-to-day situations in life, silence is a very important aspect that we tend to ignore. Look around, everything is unfolding in a natural rhythmic pattern, the trees are in no haste to grow faster, the dog and the cattle are not aiming for some higher position, and the birds do not aim to be superior. Their evolution is governed by instincts. Nobody is in a hurry except us humans. We often lack patience and expect instant outcomes for our desires. Peace cannot be experienced without surrendering to the laws of nature. We live in a physical, multidimensional outside world, thereby missing the subtle natural energies that lie within us. Our failure to understand this basic thing has affected our internal physical and mental functioning, too.

In the past, we at least tried to relax and give some time to ourselves and our family. But now we become restless after being kept away from our electronic gadgets. We try to assert our existence through our social media posts or through the comments we receive on them. We share our everyday pictures and feel offended if nobody responds to them. We have given our control to the outside world and are influenced by the negative things being shared online. Today we have huge digital communities, but no one to listen to our problems.

Digital advances are reducing our physical activity and therefore we now try to balance it by putting our mental energies into the virtual world. Computers are getting faster and we try to get maximum output by putting more time into it thereby causing mental fatigue.

Silence as Medicine

Silence is necessary for our mind and body. Here, the emphasis is on reducing the disturbances that affect our daily routine and cause distractions. The three recommended steps are;

Learning to stop

Learning to accept & let go

Learning to surrender with faith

Learning to stop

The continuous exposure to the news on the news channels, the disturbing posts on social media, and the content on television are all adding to our misery. In the name of entertainment, we are inviting long-term mental and behavioural issues. Identify the apps on your phone and PC that take up a considerable amount of your time. They are not just taking away your time but also affecting your creativity and your ability to think and perform. Delete them straight away if they add no value to your life.

Learning to accept

In the modern world, avoiding digital platforms is challenging. So, ask yourself these two questions;

1) Whether I'm using the internet and digital platforms aimlessly and allowing them to overtake my creative and thinking ability?
2) Am I using the potential of the internet and digital platforms for my self-development, value addition, and wealth creation?

This is important because we tend to ignore the effect of digital technology, which keeps our minds preoccupied. The much-desired silence can never be attained under such a mental state. We provide rest to our body, but what about the mind? Silence is the resting zone of our minds. We need a break from our thoughts. De-clutter your digital, physical and mental place. Learning to surrender with faith

The technological advances would be rapid and we may get overwhelmed with the thought of matching these advances. First of all, let us accept our limitations of not being able to match the speed of advances and not panic.

Apart from digital challenges, we would be prone to natural disasters, epidemics, water, and resource shortages brought about by climate change. During the recent COVID pandemic, we found ourselves in a helpless situation. Such situations are supposed to arise frequently in the future. The human race seems to be in no hurry to put up collective efforts to save the planet or themselves.

When things are not under your control, the best way is to surrender with faith. Let us take an example, if we add a little mud into the jar of water and keep it stirring, then the water will remain muddy. We need to stop the stirring and allow the mud to settle down for the water to gain clarity. Similarly, we need to stop the continuous stirring of the muddy (negative) thoughts that dominate our minds to experience the silence within.

Sometimes in life, we encounter moments when nothing seems to work in our favor. The only thing we can do in such a situation is to surrender with faith. This is explained in the next chapter.

A middle path that allows us to harness the potential of digital systems without getting enslaved to them is the need of the hour.

CHAPTER 26

SURRENDER WITH FAITH

Do not always try to take control of your life.
Sometimes, allow nature to do the work.

There are tough situations in life when we feel helpless and do not know whom to turn to for help. We either suffer in silence or try to fight back. We are unaware that sometimes it is better to allow nature to take control of the situation. We think that we govern things, but it is not true.

Let's take, for example, we grow crops. But do we grow them? Or they grow us!

We think that we grow crops. But in reality, they are the ones who nurture and help us in our growth.

We are not the creators. We do not control things. If we understand this and sincerely surrender before nature, then our life force attunes itself with the natural functioning of the universal energy. We need not be science students to understand the laws of nature. We just need to come out of our creator mindset and allow nature to do the work.

Let's assume, for example, what would happen if we try to interfere with nature's way of functioning in our bodies?

The heart beats on its own, the breath entering and leaving the nostrils does not require our assistance, the eye blinks, and the digestive system functions without requiring any intervention from us. The functioning of nature is amazing. Nature knows its work perfectly.

The laws of nature are the same for eternity and would remain the same forever; it is our mental energy that makes us drift away from our true nature, thereby causing problems.

There are true-life incidents where people overcame their problems by surrendering to nature.

The Story of Surrendering with Faith

This incident is about a farmer who decided to commit suicide as he was unable to repay his debts. The crop yield that year was not good, and he feared trouble and harassment from the moneylenders. Ending his life seemed to be the only option for him.

The farmer got up early in the morning and took a rope along, intending to hang himself on one of the trees on his farm. He walked towards his field; the sun was yet to rise. He could feel his racing heart and trembling body. He had not been to the field for some days due to a disturbed mindset, and as he approached the farm, he could see the plants drying due to a lack of water. The cow and the calf were overjoyed to see their master as they were awaiting their fodder. He could sense the effect of his absence on his farm. The plants and animals were awaiting him desperately.

He immediately got down to work and provided fodder to the cattle and water to the plants. As his hands gently touched the plants and cattle, tears began to roll down his cheeks..

"They need you. Your family needs you," he muttered to himself.

Unsure about what to do next, he went into the open space in the centre of the farm. He had no instant solution. Unsure about what to do, he spontaneously lay down on the earth as if his whole body was embracing Mother Earth. Every atom of his shivering body was asking for help from the earth and existence. This was the moment of total surrender. He remained still for a few moments and then got up, fully determined, and charged up to take on the challenges of life. As he arose, he could see the sun slowly rising above the horizon. He took this as an assurance of a bright new beginning. The birds were singing merrily, and the breeze was caressing his body.

Once you accept your limitations and surrender, the ego takes a back seat, the mind becomes clear and receptive to newer ideas.

The farmer not only managed to pay back his debts but also managed to give himself and his family a decent life.

Our existence in this world is the result of the coming together of different elements of the universe. We can attune with this source of ours by following the daily practice of expressing gratitude through compassion, charity, and meditation. These are ways to reconnect with our source of existence. Once you are attuned, it becomes easier to allow the laws of nature to take care. Just like a radio, which can be tuned by adjusting to the desired frequency, we too can harness the powers of nature.

Way to Experience Inner Silence

Being a good listener.
Spending more time with nature.
Through Meditation.
By practising mindfulness.

For a detailed understanding, refer to the author's other life-changing book 'The Power of Metta & Mindfulness Mefitation"

CHAPTER 27

THE BEGINNING

Play the game of life well.

Dear reader,

Whole-hearted Metta to you. Metta is a genuine and earnest wish for the happiness of all beings. We are into the final chapter of this book & if you find the contents helpful, then the credit for its success goes to you. This is because the extent of effectiveness of the book will depend on the understanding of the concepts and their implementation. If there are any shortcomings in the book, then the fault lies with me. However, let me assure you that the book is written with the pure intention to help you all with the tools and techniques that I have personally used in my life and have achieved great results with.

The recipe for success is a mixture of various ingredients and varies as per the mindset from person to person. Hence, your success recipe differs from any other person's. There is no single formula for success, and there is no instant formula either. Hence, this book doesn't make any tall claims and asks its readers to use discretion.

Let us now summarize some of the important points in this book. One of the primary purposes of this book is to decide our priorities in life. What should be the sequence of our priorities? What do I want first? Riches, relationships, power, or what else? Preferences may vary from person to person. Most of us prioritize money, but understand that being wealthy is a need and should not be our lifelong priority.

Whatever your present need may be, our priority should be FREEDOM, and achieving that freedom at the earliest should be my priority. Most of us spend a significant portion of our lives searching for financial stability, and therefore, we chase money out of either 'need or greed' throughout our lives. So, learning to stop our money chase at the right time and choosing to 'live' is the biggest challenge to overcome.

What is the value of your freedom?

This appears to be an absurd question because we are often told that life cannot be valued in terms of materialistic wealth. But didn't we spend our lives running after money? We continue to chase money because we are unsure about the amount that is sufficient to sustain a decent and fulfilling life. We often forget to pause and appreciate the simple beauty that life offers. Until we learn to balance the materialistic part of our life with the spiritualistic one, it will not be possible to live a life of contentment. We carry many tensions in our lives, and earning money is the major one among all. Further, most of our tensions are related to a lack of money. Hence, once we take care of the money part, we can concentrate on other parameters of life.

Creating Wealth

Since wealth creation takes away a major chunk of our lives, a plan to earn the required wealth in a time-bound manner is necessary. Hence, decide the amount of money that would be sufficient to take care of all your family's needs and to enable you to lead a comfortable life. Work out and earn that amount in a time-bound manner. The needs and requirements differ from person to person and from age to age. The requirements of a young person may differ from those of an old one. It is an individual choice, so don't bother about what the world would desire. Think about yourself and decide the amount and the timeframe within which you intend to achieve that goal.

An important point to be noted- A particular amount of money may appear huge today and we may fail to work out the exact projected amount we may need after particular years (say 10 years). Let me give an example of how you can calculate your future wealth projection;

Let's take an example of a person earning an annual income of say Rs. 12,00000/- (i.e., Rs one lakh per month). He is presently 45 years of age and wants to retire after 10 years (at the age of 55). What would be his projected income then?

The formula to calculate this is;

Present income x (1+%of income rise per year) ^years to retirement.

His present income is Rs. 1200000

Projected per-year income rise is assumed as 10%

Years to retirement are 10

His projected annual income after 10 years would be 1200000x (1+10%) ^10

=1200000x (1.1) ^10 =3112490

You may accordingly decide the money that would suffice for your future as per your requirements and goals.

Decide the priorities of your life. Find out what you want and get it done within a stipulated time

If you lack riches, decide the amount of lifetime money you need to support yourself and your family to live a decent life or even a lavish life. But in any case, the time frame for achieving those riches should be clear in your mind. Invest some part of the earned money in a passive income source and let it grow. One should not work throughout life and later lament not utilizing those riches due to old age. In today's digital and AI age, it has become easier to earn money even while sleeping. It has become easier to launch your product or courses with the help of free tools available online. The required investment comes at a minimal cost.

Once you have no financial issues, incorporating gratitude, compassion, charity, and meditation in your life will balance it with peace and harmony. The greed for never-ending materialistic needs will subside. Invest some part of the available wealth in passive income sources such that the money will continue to grow even while you sleep. Lead a meaningful, prosperous life rather than a financially rich one.

Create a time-bound plan and make it happen; a life of freedom. Live life on your terms and conditions, and by doing things that enliven you. Once you conquer the challenge of building wealth, ensure that money itself never turns into a barrier on your path to true freedom.

Learn to Stop and Enjoy Life

At the core of all our pursuits lies a genuine longing for happiness. Why do we need money? To become happy, obviously. But if we continue to chase money even after having sufficient riches, then we are compromising our happiness. The ultimate aim of life is joy, and wealth simply serves as one of the means to help us experience it. Also, our happiness is directly proportional to the happiness we create in the lives of others.

Tackle the Problem

We all have problems in life. If the problem is manageable, do not keep it lingering. Resolving it may be difficult, but try the techniques provided in the book as they may help tide you over that difficulty. If the problem is beyond your control, for example, being physically challenged, then try to end the sorrow and misery associated with that trauma. In any case, do not allow any problem to come in your freedom's way. Rise above and liberate yourself by rising above the sorrow and limitations. Don't wait for the suffering to end. Grief does not end by itself. Learn to create a moment of happiness in between, and you will find the miseries slowly fading away. Drop by drop, fill yourself with such moments, and moments of happiness will overtake the moments of misery. It takes only a drop of lemon to spoil the milk and only a drop of essence to make it fragrant. It is up to you to choose the type of drop you want to add.

Make the End Blissful

Remember, a person on his deathbed does not ask for an empire or wealth but asks for a few more breaths. At the very last moment, we realise the importance of our breath, our life. Most of us die unhappily. As our last moment approaches, the memories of our whole life quickly flash before our eyes. We regret the lost opportunities. Life could have been bliss, a blessing to rejoice in, but we got distracted and failed to live to our fullest.

Also, I remind myself of the Dalai Lama's words,

'My existence is for mutual upliftment of myself and others.'

Hence, remember to keep a share of your wealth for charity. Your freedom will be more wholesome if it includes the deeds of doing well to others.

From the many great human souls that have graced this world to an ordinary human being like me, it has been a personal experience that the inclusion of gratitude, compassion, charity, and meditation forms a fullproof plan for a happy, blissful, and successful life.

Scientific studies have proved that happiness more often leads to success rather than the other way around. Learn to create happiness, and things begin to change.

Final Spark

A seed planted in soil may or may not germinate for various reasons, but a thought planted in the mind will always result.

Remember, the mind is amazing as well as challenging. It challenges you, but if you harness its power, it can amaze you with limitless possibilities.

It is said that if we sincerely and wholeheartedly pray for the well-being and happiness of others, then existence also aids us in our progress towards the desired destination.

May you be blessed!
May you receive abundance and prosperity!
May you be free from sorrows and miseries!
May you be blessed with good physical and mental health!
May you be liberated!

Upcoming Books from Author Gyan Panpatil

1) The Power of Metta and Mindfulness Meditation.

Life-Changing Techniques to Use Mind and Heart for Healing, Peace, and Inner Strength

2) Meditation On-the-Go, Anywhere Anytime

50+ Quick Meditation Techniques for Stress Relief, Focus, and Inner Calm